T

THE ODDS AGAINST

Cathy,
Find your advantage!

By
Keith Harris

[signature]

Copyright 2019

Edited by John Fotia

Table of Contents

A Note from the author   5

Foreword by Ken Bozeman   9

The Symphony of Life   11

Introduction   13

The Journey Begins   17

Finding the Advantage   21

Overcoming Obstacles   31

Exploration   35

Living your Dream   43

Risk versus Reward   59

Listen to your Body   67

Mindset   77

Loss   77

Gratitude   91

Dealing with Rejection   97

Nerves and Stage Fright   107

Effort and Reward   115

Love Yourself   119

The Odds Against

A Note from the Author

From my journal—July 8, 2006.

> I am finding more and more in life whenever I don't trust my gut, that inner voice, I wish later I had listened.

Why do we struggle so much when it comes to accepting our truest self? We struggle because we are unique, and unique is often mistaken for weird. I am a unique person. I wrestle with that every day. Being unique is difficult because we don't come with a handbook. You are not born with a set of "how to" instructions. So "unique" is tossed aside and replaced with "weird." The result is that we close ourselves off and never find our purpose in life. Worse yet, we stop paying attention to who we are and focus solely on what we do. If society sees us doing the right thing then we won't be weird. Right? We also will no longer be unique.

Let's explore:

Do you feel misunderstood and disregarded?
Do you or someone you love have a learning disability?
Do you often get up on the wrong side of the bed?
Do you have an employee or student you struggle to understand or motivate?
Do you find yourself going through life wondering if you are making a difference?
Are you quick to judge yourself negatively?
Does *supposed to be* not feel like what you *thought it would be*?
Are you living your life with purpose, on purpose?

I'll bet you answered yes to at least one of these questions. Society teaches us to avoid these topics. Instead, we are given a social checklist that will ensure that we are seen as successful. But what is normal? What is success? And who gets to define it? If *normal* does not fit inside your skin then you will not be truly happy, even if you follow every social rule to perfection.

What I offer here is not a self-help book with a "to-do" list. It is certainly not a *"how-to"* formula. In fact, in some parts, it might be closer to a *"how-not-to"* formula. Basically, it is my autobiography (so far) with some perspectives and life lessons that might be of help to you. As with all good stories there is a twist in this one. It can be easy getting so caught up in the daily rat race, focusing on goals, dreams, and competitions that we quite literally forget where we are standing. And more tragically, why we are standing there. This frustration often brings motivation and progress to a grinding and painful halt.

Goals and dreams are exciting but the purpose of this book is more internal. What purpose in life drove you to those dreams in the first place? First and foremost, appreciate who you are, listen to that voice deep inside you that often defies logic and say thank you for every day no matter what happens.

I don't consider myself to be extraordinary. In fact, I struggled with the idea of sharing my story. But I believe that I offer a perspective that illustrates how life itself is extraordinary. It doesn't matter who you are or where you come from. If you gain a new appreciation of that, I will consider this effort a massive success.

A lot of people have helped me along the way. So many that it would not be possible to mention them all in this book. But I want to stress the importance of mentors. These are the people who are part of life-changing moments. Sometimes it's a stranger offering a smile, and sometimes (as you will see in this book) it is someone who fixes our voices. I talk a lot about mentors. I am grateful for their love and the lessons they impart because without their care and dedication I would not have had the opportunity to share my story.

Thank you for reading.

From my journal—December 2, 2004.

> I have been getting that feeling again that I have a book in me. I still have no idea what it's about or when I'll write it... I just keep getting the feeling that I have a book in me. I hope it'll come in time. Maybe writing in this journal will help bring it out.

Kenneth Bozeman and Keith Harris after performing a recital together, Door County, WI, 2008.

Keith Harris in my very first Barbershop tuxedo 1984.

Foreword

It is the hope and goal of any true educator that every child succeed. There is a growing acknowledgement within the education community that students with special challenges can both progress and succeed if given accommodations appropriate for their learning process. The challenge is determining what adjustments are needed and appropriate and how best to stimulate the will to succeed in students that have become convinced that they cannot. Keith Harris' story gives us a needed example, both of his creative, supportive mentors, and of his own courageous persistence.

Keith Harris was a vocal performance and music education double major at Lawrence University Conservatory of Music in Appleton, Wisconsin in the mid-1990s. I was his voice professor during his time there, and our relationship continued after his graduation. I am honored to report that we became good friends. That was an easy transition, in part, frankly, because Keith was a terrific student to teach. He had a beautiful instrument and an innate expressive musicality. More to the point though is the fact that Keith had a terrific "can do," cooperative attitude. He was not merely receptive, he eagerly invited correction and guidance, so much so that I have since used Keith with some frequency as an example of the kind of approach that results in great progress. In fact, Keith was so resilient and receptive of guidance that I could proceed frankly and efficiently, without wasting precious lesson time with undue concern about discouraging him. He was like the inflatable boxing clowns of my childhood that would always pop back up for more, no matter the critique you hit them with! This degree of resilience is atypical. Having now read Keith's story and learned from it many things I had not known when he was my student, I have a better understanding of how that quality of character evolved. Keith grew through adversity, with strong parental support, and with crucial guidance by insightful individuals along the way, support and guidance upon which Keith himself capitalized and built.

A number of years after his graduation, Keith sent me a recording of his singing and asked for my feedback. Consistent with his nature, his accompanying letter spoke positively of how he felt things were going—he was never a complainer. Unfortunately, upon listening to the recording, I heard some technical deterioration emerging in his approach to the *passaggio* into the upper voice—a key element for successful singing. My letter in response was difficult to write, but I knew Keith wanted and expected an honest evaluation. His initial reaction was a respectful, "This may be the one time when we have to agree to disagree." A few weeks later, Keith wrote again, reporting that his other two main mentors had agreed with my concerns, and that he was therefore making important changes in guidance to get back on a good path. The book you are reading reports how such willingness to admit need for the help from trusted others, and then to take appropriate action in response—especially to difficult feedback—can lead to career success like that which Keith has since enjoyed. His example and the advice he offers come from one who has responded to life's challenges with healthy adjustment.

Now Keith is able to offer credible, sage counsel to the journey of others. I recommend that you read Keith's story with an open mind and spirit, and absorb as much of his positive approach as you can. While each person's path through adversity will be unique, as will whatever form each person's success takes, reading of how a fellow pilgrim made his way through life's challenges will encourage you on your own journey, especially when you realize that though, yes, Keith is special, we are each unique, with our own special gifts, and with as yet unrealized great potential.

December, 2018

Kenneth Bozeman
Frank C. Shattuck Professor of Music
Lawrence University Conservatory of Music

The Symphony of Life

Are you playing your instrument in the symphony of life? Living in harmony is playing your instrument. Are there difficult passages to play? Oh, yes. Choosing to play does not mean one is an immediate master. But the benefits far outweigh the challenges. The symphony of life pays well, has a great health plan, and an unlimited source of experiences. Let's not judge those experiences. All music is welcome.

How does one deal with another who does not wish to play in the symphony, plays poorly, or focuses their time only telling others how to play? The most powerful enjoyment and influence comes from living and playing by example. We are not to boast about our skills or the mastery of our instrument. Neither should we live in fear that we do not have the skills to perfect our instrument. All that is required is a desire to play. Play for the love of playing, and be playful in your sorrow and in your joy. Those who wish not to play in the symphony will fade away and those who love harmony will become your most beloved allies.

The symphony truly is perfect. The instruments are vast and unlimited. Membership is unlimited. But you must choose to play. Desire is the membership fee. No one can play for you. You must pick out your instrument, practice each day, and the music will take you on the most unexpected and magnificent adventure.

John Eshelman (my grandfather) with the trumpet he later gave to me, 1938.

Keith Harris—Cauldwell, WI, 1984.

Introduction

About 15 years after I graduated from college I learned that not only was I almost not accepted into the school where I got my degree, but that my acceptance was highly controversial. I also discovered that my success in the program helped change the application process for future students.

I'm dyslexic. If you grew up in the 1980s this basically meant you were slow, or as I felt, *dumb*. How slow was I? When I was in the third grade my teacher recommended moving me from the lowest level reading group to a group with intellectual and developmental disabilities.

My mom, who is also dyslexic, had a different idea. She insisted that I be moved to the regular level reading group. My teacher pushed back, warning her that the move would be setting me up for failure. Mom fired back with, "I know my son. He's not dumb. He needs time to figure things out. And as his teacher, your job is to give him that time."

Go mom!

I can see where my teacher was coming from. I was insecure because I felt dumb and was struggling to understand how to function in the world. My response was to fight. I had a short fuse and a hot temper. Kids who picked on me got punched. Patience and tolerance were not on my radar. I was thin skinned and responded violently to criticism. Fights were a regular event for me on the playground. In fact, my parents were almost sued for the cost of dental work after I knocked out a kid's tooth. Fortunately, the lost tooth was a baby tooth and both parents agreed that it takes two to fight. Was I a bully? No, that would require me to be a good fighter and for kids to be scared of me. My temper was a form of entertainment, which only made things worse. Kids enjoyed getting a rise out of the weird kid. I was not winning "King of the Hill." I was overwhelmed and felt out of place and insecure.

So when my mother said to my teacher that her son, the one who acts like he has mad cow disease on the playground, is a smart kid who has great potential, I can understand why my teacher didn't see it right away.

Nevertheless, I was moved to the regular level reading group and a remarkable thing happened. My grades stayed the same. I was getting a D in the lowest level group and got a D in the regular reading group. It wasn't the information I couldn't understand. I struggled with comprehension in general. Imagine going through life without comprehension skills. I always felt lost.

What had happened with my mother's dyslexia? She finished her undergraduate work when I was young and was told not to pursue graduate school because she was not smart enough and would fail. Mom never forgot what that felt like, and she was determined to prevent my school from passing that wounding message on to me.

Passing classes was so difficult that my parents came to celebrate a C. Most kids get ice cream for straight A's but I got ice cream for no D's. If someone told me then that my future would consist of memorizing hundreds of pages of music, sometimes atonal music, with libretti in French, German, Italian, and even Latin, it's likely I would have had a nervous breakdown. But music became my escape and biggest inspiration.

When I was nine years old, I joined a Barbershop Harmony chorus that was directed by my father and where I was treated as one of the guys. It was the one place where I was one of the cool kids. I was allowed to participate in the chorus as long as I got all C's or better. It was my favorite event of the week. Music gave me a sense of purpose and that is the reason I am a professional singer today.

What is a sense of purpose? Purpose: a person's sense of resolve or determination.

Purpose is defined by who you are and not by what you do. It is the fire that makes getting out of bed each day worthwhile. It's the light in your eyes that makes you inimitable. It's the outlet or the muse that you find most rewarding and most painful. For example, singing well elevates my spirit; singing poorly feels like a punishment. But singing is not my purpose. Singing provides the window through which purpose is discovered. Purpose is the inspiration; greater than the sum of its parts. It defies logic. Find your purpose, and life's weapons of opposition will create a path upon which you can walk. In fact, eventually you will realize the weapons of opposition are a gift; a gift designed to keep you on track. On purpose.

Susan May
Cauldwell, WI, 1986.

Keith Harris and Karen Hassey,
8th grade graduation, Washington
Cauldwell School, WI, 1989.

The Journey Begins

> When I was five years old my mother told me happiness was the key to life. When I went to school, they asked me what I wanted to be when I grew up. I wrote down "happy." They told me I didn't understand the assignment. I told them they didn't understand life. ~ John Lennon

According to popular opinion, all stories should start at the beginning. Let's begin with mine. I was born on August 13, 1975 in Elgin, Illinois, a small unassuming town outside of Chicago. We moved a couple times in my first year-and-a-half of life before landing in Janesville, Wisconsin, the town that I would call home until age 11.

My father, Roger, was 26 and my mother, Susan, was 23 when I was born and when I reached those ages I thought, "what were they thinking?" I still think I am too young to have kids. I am quite happy being the neighborhood uncle. To many of the neighbors I am known as "Tio Keith."

Dad spent most of his working life as a Claims Adjuster for American Family Insurance. Until I was in the fourth grade mom was a homemaker. Little brother Paul came along three-and-a-half years later. I remember mom telling me that the family was getting a new addition. Excited, I stated that I wanted a pony. She responded with, "How about a brother or a sister?" I said I'd take a brother if I had to but I'd prefer a pony. Mom informed me we might not get that choice but she'd do her best.

My brother came home (as all babies do) wrapped in a blanket and sleeping. I frowned in confusion and asked, "Is that all he does?" I would have to wait a few years for a playmate. Eventually, we conquered the world together in our backyard, survived epic fights that only brothers can brag about, shared the stage in three championship Barbershop quartets, and remain close friends. As young, active kids who loved to pick on each other (and sometimes even hurt each other on purpose), it could be hard to tell when the wrestling was for fun and when the fight was real. We are both quite competitive. The complaint that might be the all-time winner for silencing my parents came from my brother during a family vacation when, after a long car ride, he yelled, "He's breathing my air!"

My brother is also the keeper of "The Contract." The Contract was signed when my brother and I were kids. After a more impressive round of fighting (and possibly in an effort to avoid more broken furniture), we were inspired to write The Contract which states that when I am 70 years old and my brother is 67 we will wrestle. The winner will take home a cool $20 cash. Have no fear my dear reader, I absolutely plan to win that $20.

I had what I like to call a *real* childhood. Janesville was a nice town in which to grow up. It was small, safe, and homes with backyards were affordable. I had lots of friends in the neighborhood. No, I was not a child prodigy who practiced music eight hours a day after school. In fact, because my parents started the family when they were young they didn't have the money for music lessons. I never feared that I would go unfed, but most of my clothes were second hand and my parents found inventive ways to keep me busy with activities that were inexpensive or free. I participated in sports, was a member of the Cub Scouts, sang in church choirs, and we always had a dog in the house. Although it was not a *perfect* childhood, it was an ideal foundation for an artist. A simple, lower-middle-class, Midwestern life provided the foundation and work ethic required to keep sane while maintaining a grueling schedule and traveling around the world singing.

My dad's other hobby besides Barbershop was cars. As such, I grew up working with my hands. Years later, I found that my love for working in the garage was based on the fact that I am a "visual learner." Being able to *see* how things work makes sense to my brain, as opposed to simply reading about or having someone tell me about it. Because of this, I developed a life-long appreciation (or what my wife calls, a healthy obsession) for cars and beautiful craftsmanship. Working on cars is amazing because you see the results of your efforts immediately. Once a project is completed you can count the hours and cut fingers that went into a beautifully finished project. Car guys brag about bruises in the garage. Why not elsewhere in life too? I didn't realize at the time how much that sense of satisfaction would play into my work ethic as I got older.

Along with working with my hands I was a busy body. I still am. I think if I had been born ten years later I probably would have been a candidate for Ritalin. Fortunately, I was simply considered "hyper" and, as such, my parents thought the best medicine for me was playing in the yard. I have never been good at sitting still, but my parents were right; I didn't need to be fixed or controlled. I needed to learn how to burn off some energy. Eventually, I learned how to focus this massive outlet of energy and use it in more productive ways. I didn't need to turn my home into a jungle.

All in all, it seems like basically a normal childhood right? Not completely. One of my favorite foods was liver and onions. To this day my mom still has no idea what was wrong with my tongue. I thought she made it because I liked it and she says she made it because it was cheap and easy. I will admit I do not eat liver and onions today.

Seated in the front row center, Keith Harris with the Northbrook Barbershop Chorus, Peoria, IL, 1987.

Finding the Advantage

> Not that there won't continue to be challenges, but more and more they'll be understood as gifts that ultimately reveal previously unrecognized shortcuts forward.[1]

My fourth grade year in school was life changing. So many things happened all at once. This was the year my mom started seminary, the year I joined the Barbershop Harmony Society, and the first time I got a sense that maybe I was not *dumb*.

Once my brother and I were in grade school, mom decided that it was time to finish her degree and start her own career. She began in social work which, while rewarding, was not the right fit. When she announced that she would pursue a career in Ministry, my father fell out of his chair. Ignoring the advice of that undergraduate counselor who said she was not smart enough for graduate school, mom applied and was accepted to Garret Evangelical Theological Seminary on the campus of Northwestern University in Evanston, Illinois where she went on to earn her Masters in Divinity.

The drive from Janesville to Evanston takes about two hours depending on traffic. Commuting to classes each day was impossible. This meant mom spent four days a week at school living in the dorms. She came home on the weekends to study, finish homework, and have a little family time. This also meant the three guys had to live alone most of the week and my brother and I had to help out around the house. In addition to school and homework we had chores.

---

[1] *The Top Ten Things Dead People Want to Tell YOU* (2014). Mike Dooley. Hay House, Carlsbad, California. ©Mike Dooley, www.tut.com

One of my jobs was to do the dishes. We didn't have a dishwasher; I was the dishwasher. This meant I had to wash an entire day's worth of dishes every night after dinner. This often included the casserole dish. I hated washing the casserole dish. That baked on junk never seemed to come off.

The importance of doing the dishes was underscored after I let the dirty dishes sit overnight in the kitchen sink. The next morning, the ants made their appearance. I'm not talking about a few ants. Family breakfast was attended by an entire city of ants. In fact, I think all the ants in Janesville were invited to the party. It was disgusting. It freaked me out so much that I wasn't able to clean up the mess. My parents assisted in the clean-up and were much stricter about my work schedule after that.

This is also the year my musical life took on a huge progression. In Janesville, kids were encouraged to take up an instrument in the fourth grade. I was introduced to the trumpet during the summer before school started. While visiting my grandparents on my mother's side in Iowa City, Grandpa John pulled out his trumpet—the one he played in World War II. It hadn't seen the light of day in years. The horn was well traveled as he was stationed in the South Pacific. The finish was in rough shape, the case was pretty beaten up, and I could hardly make a sound. I loved it. The trumpet was my instrument of choice, and I was excited to have my own instrument. Beyond playing the trumpet, I asked my grandfather what he did in World War II. He asked me, "Do you like the show MASH?"

"Yes," I replied.
He smiled, "I was Radar."

Singers are often ridiculed for their lack of rhythmic ability or responsibility. Playing the trumpet gave me an early start in reading music and a greater appreciation for orchestration and rhythm. After a frustrating rehearsal, a conductor once asked me, "What brass instrument did you play?"

"The trumpet," I replied.

"I knew it," he fired back. "You're the only damn singer on stage with any sense of rhythm. You, my friend, have a very bright future ahead of you." The Maestro had been a trombone player with the Metropolitan Opera Orchestra.

All singers need to play some sort of instrument. The piano is certainly the most logical choice and so I learned to play. I still play, albeit poorly. Nevertheless, having some basic piano skills allows me to learn music accurately on my own. That saves tons of money. Playing an instrument also teaches discipline that requires sticking to a practice routine. Having a creative outlet that fosters discipline is a valuable foundation for professionals in all fields of study.

The old trumpet? It is a 1929 Martin. The old school guys love this horn. The bore is smaller than the modern classical horns making it a classic representation of the big band era. My grandparents had it completely re-silvered and rebuilt for me before high school. It looked brand new and played even better. While the horn, once again, hasn't seen the light of day in years, I still own it and always will.

As I mentioned earlier, it was during my fourth-grade year that I joined the Barbershop Harmony Society. This changed my life as a singer forever, and the best part is that it all happened by accident. It's almost as if fate stepped in to make sure that I would spend my life as a singer. My parents could not find a baby sitter one evening so my brother went with my mom to her event, and I went to a Barbershop rehearsal with my dad. It was an all-male, a cappella chorus singing four-part harmony. What a sound! The thing that makes Barbershop unique is that the melody line is in the second tenor also known as the "Lead" line. Being a part of that a cappella sound is invigorating.

As long as I was there why not sing? My dad was the director of the chorus so he put me in the tenor section. The range was kind of low for me because my voice had not yet changed. I was a boy soprano. But it was the highest vocal part they offered. I loved it and was hooked immediately. The members of the chorus loved when I accidentally sang the tenor part up an octave because it sounded like a really loud overtone. In case you are not familiar with overtones they are the high ringy sound in a singer's voice. When many voices work together the ring can be extraordinary and Barbershop singers live for it. Monks were reputed to love this sound as well, and when they heard it they claimed that when they sounded good the angles sang along.

When we got home from rehearsal my dad told my mom that their sitter problems were solved because I loved singing Barbershop. In fact, I was even pretty good at it. Being in a men's chorus made me grow up quickly. The rules were straightforward. If you were going to sing in a group with adults you had to act like an adult. To my surprise the adults treated me the same way. And if you get to stay out late for rehearsal you have to get out of bed and make it to school on time. NO PROBLEM! I loved singing so much I would have jumped through almost any hoop to stay in Barbershop. It was my favorite event of the week.

Singing gave me a sense of purpose or from a fourth grader's point of view, made me feel cool. Feeling cool, even for only one rehearsal a week, gave me just enough energy to start taking on dyslexia.

> Dyslexia: a general term for disorders that involve difficulty in learning to read or interpret words, letters, and other symbols, but that do not affect general intelligence.

Did you notice what it says in that last section? *Does not affect general intelligence.* I never actually read a definition of dyslexia until I was out of college. How unfortunate.

Dyslexia, my *disability* as it was popularly referred to, is kind of like having your brain in a scrambler. You feel confused easily and often. Words literally move around the page while you are reading them. You can read a paragraph over and over and still have no comprehension of what you have read. Yet I was not illiterate. Numbers come out backwards. I was pretty good at and enjoyed math. I often had the right answer on assignments if you took into consideration that I may have reversed a couple of numbers. Even today, I still can't spell to save my soul because sounding it out in English doesn't really work. When you add this all up it's easy to see why I actually thought I was dumb.

This poem by Sally Gardner sums it up pretty well.

Disobey Me[2]
They told me I was dyslexic
it didn't describe me
belonged in the library
of words I can't spell
no matter how many times they tell
you just try harder sound it out
simple when you think about
it. Stop giving me the third degree
don't put me down
don't make me fret
I can't learn my alphabet
it doesn't go in any logical order
the stress gives me attention deficit disorder
at school I wanted to go it alone
they told me that's unwise
they called me unteacheable
I was unreachable
stuck in the classroom, broken by rules, by buttons
and ties.
But I don't like the little words they always disobey
me
the does doses up and is higher than a dude should be
So they tested me
they corrected me

---

[2] *Everything is Spherical: An Anthology of Dyslexic Writers* (2014). Naomi Folb. RASP Publisher.

and found my results poor
and told me I wasn't concentrating
they expected more.
I tried to get along
I never made the score
And I think about Chaucer in those freedom days
when no one found your spelling faulty for the extra
Es and As
Mr. Shakespeare I wonder would they let him write
his plays?
Oh woe is me
might just be
graffiti in a bog
And Hamlet the name
he called his prize-fighter dog
But I don't like the little words they always disobey
me
the doe doses dope and is higher than a do should be
You say that you're a writer
but that's absurd
how do you write
if you cannot spell the words?
listen, it's not the way I spell
that makes me want to write
It's the way I see the world
That makes me want to fight
I challenge you – see the words as I do
feel them sting your skin
the meaning often shocking
the way the nib goes in
to relish discombobulate not to moderate your
passion
not to murder language in an artificial fashion
words are our servants
we are not their slaves
it matters not if we spell them wrong it matters what

they say
But I don't like the little words they always disobey
me
the does doses dope and is higher than a dough
should be.

The frustration of constantly struggling to understand almost everything released itself in the form of anger. I fought with everything and everyone in sight. I got into fights on the playground, punched walls, broke toys, and because I had a healthy voice, made plenty of noise when I yelled. One time, I even kicked the keys off the keyboard of our family's Tandy 1000 Radio Shack computer because I kept losing the game I was playing.

My fourth grade teacher began the process of teaching me how to learn, and the side benefit was that my temper began to be curbed. My *disability* ultimately became an asset because it forced me to learn how to learn—and that is a very powerful tool.

Test taking was always where my grades took their biggest dive. I struggled with test taking. My fourth grade teacher, Mr. Littlejohn, made it his mission to prove to me that I could, in fact, learn the needed material for a test and pass that test. Our conversation went something like this:

"Mr. Harris, would you stay after class please?"
"Yes sir."
"How are things at home Keith?"
"Fine," I said shuffling my feet.

Mr. Littlejohn smiled and continued.

"Your mom is doing well in seminary?"
"Yeah, she got straight A's again."
"She still spends the week at Seminary and comes home on the weekends?"
"Yup."

"So you, your bother, and your dad take care of the house during the week?"

"Yeah, my job is the dishes."

Now that the small talk was out of the way Mr. Littlejohn got down to business.

"You're a good kid and I want to help you with your history exams. You're well aware the last three have not gone so well?"

"I know. I tried to study but ..."

He was amazingly calm and reassuring.

"I would like to suggest we try something."

And then it seemed that maybe he wasn't so reassuring. This one phrase made my heart race. What was he going to say? All I could think of was that I was in trouble. You only get held after class if you're in trouble. Was he going to move me to the lowest level group? Hold me back a year? Push me back to third grade? Was I going to have to defend myself—all by myself? And how would I do that if I really was—a *dumb* kid. Maybe I did deserve to be moved or held back. But how embarrassing! All my friends would make fun of me. I saw how mean kids were to another kid who failed third grade and was held back. I was absolutely frozen.

Mr. Littlejohn deepened his focus.

"I think we should have you take the test again."

"You mean, now?"

"No, tomorrow; and the day after, and the day after that if we need to, until you pass."

"I don't understand."

"Exactly! And we're going to make sure that you do."

Amazing! He was going to prove to me that I could pass these tests by allowing me to take them as many times as needed. For some kids, this would be the perfect scam, right? How often do you get pulled over for speeding and simply say to the officer, "Oh, sorry about that. Let me take a U-turn and try that again."

But his mission became much more powerful than proving I could pass a test. He showed me what I could accomplish by learning how to focus my efforts.

> Notice that those thoughts are now conscious, and that no matter how many times you've failed, it's possible to succeed.[3]

What does that mean?

Well, when you think you are dumb you think you've been dealt a bad hand and you'll always be the weird kid in the room. Have you ever felt like the weird kid in the room? Of course. We all know what that feels like. But somehow this helped me discover two things:

1. Time is the one thing that everyone gets the same amount of no matter who you are or what your background is; and
2. I could decide how to spend that time.

So, my effort, more than any other gift, was my biggest ally. By removing test anxiety, and giving me the safety net of retaking the tests, I was given the freedom to learn *how* to learn. What did it take to unscramble my brain? Many years later, I realized that I'm actually pretty smart. Obviously, Mr. Littlejohn already knew this and he made sure that I wasn't held back in school.

But unscrambling my brain was like getting into a safe filled with money—there was a complex combination. Because I wasn't born with an instruction manual, figuring out that combination was a long, and often frustrating, process. The next major

---

[3] *The Healing Power of Negative Thoughts and Uncomfortable Sensations* (The Thought Exchange) (2015). David Friedman. Library Tales Publishing.

breakthrough came in the sixth grade. That's when my cousin Kevin came for a visit and gave serious definition to my educational style.

Before we get to that, however, one last note about Mr. Littlejohn. After I was accepted to college, I visited my grade school to see my teachers. They all said they remembered me. I'm pretty sure most of them were just being nice, but they did seem happy to receive a positive update from a former student. But I could not find Mr. Littlejohn. I asked everyone where I might find him. They knew he was in the building but none of them knew where. It felt like a scene from a movie. I searched the corridors and finally found him. The last teacher I talked to was the one teacher I really wanted to see. The climax of my visit was saved for last.

He had just finished a lesson in the gym. I introduced myself.

"I know you have a lot of students so I don't expect you to remember me but I want to thank you." He smiled.

"Of course I remember you Keith. Is your mom still in Ministry?" You could have knocked me over with a feather. He really did remember me! I explained how his teaching turned my life around and how I was going to college to study music. Any teacher reading this knows exactly what he said. I made his entire day, month, and year. Never underestimate the power of "Thank You."

Tradition and convention provide a basic structure for education. Mr. Littlejohn was creative enough to understand that the classroom testing tradition was only a starting point and is not effective for all students. Had he left it to convention and the normal process I would have failed fourth grade. Had he tailored my exam situation for the entire class in order to make it *fair*, it might not have worked for some of them. Every person is unique and sometimes the least logical or traditional solutions are the perfect solutions. Take the test again. You just might be smarter than you think.

Overcoming Obstacles

The next major leap in my educational journey and the one that would offer the most defined direction came from Cousin Kevin. That is not his nickname. He's actually my cousin. How removed? I lose track of the math and not because I am dyslexic. His grandmother and my grandmother were sisters, which makes his mom and my dad cousins. That makes us cousins. We were always good buddies.

Kevin is about 15 years older than me. He returned from a two-year mission trip to Chile. He often came to visit over the years and I was excited to see him again because it had been a long time since we were together. His personality is that of a big brother. Because I was the big brother in my house, Kevin was like an adopted big brother. Make that a big brother with a great sense of humor—a quick wit. You had to stay sharp around Kevin.

Basketball might be Kevin's greatest hobby (long legs and an ability to jump don't seem to run in the family), but learning styles and education are his true gifts. He is still a corporate educator today. Kevin changed my life by figuring out that I am a visual learner. What does that mean? It means that I like picture books. But did you know that all books can become picture books with a little imagination?

By the time I had reached the sixth grade, I was doing fairly well in most of my classes but I was expecting a big, fat, solid F in social studies. The class didn't make sense to me and I was completely lost. Report cards had not come out yet so my Barbershop nights were safe—for the moment. But without Kevin a magnificent disaster was on the horizon.

At the time of Kevin's visit, I was studying for a history test in which I had to learn all the capital cities of the European countries. This was not going well, and I really didn't understand why the information was important. I wrote out a list in two columns with the countries on one side and the cities on the other. I ran down the list and back to the top but nothing stuck. I could not remember a single combination of countries and cities. I became frustrated, my temper was flaring, and the process was exhausting. The result was that I became complacent. I just didn't care and I wanted to quit. Because I had not developed any problem solving skills, it would have been easy to write me off as the bad kid with no potential.

Kevin asked what I was working on in school and offered to help me study for my exam. I thought "Really? You want to help with my homework?" I thought it was kind of nerdy but, why not? Clearly, I wasn't making any progress on my own.

Kevin asked me to explain the process I was using. I told him about my efforts as explained above, but admitted that I didn't really have one. That's when Kevin said, "Let's get a map."

The map was large enough to cover most of the desk and was very colorful. Each country was displayed in a different color. Not long after, I discovered that this would be a key factor in my upcoming exam. We started by learning the capital cities for just three countries. The "fingers" as I called them were Norway, Sweden, and Finland. Kevin made sure we started small, breaking off the project into bite-sized chunks that would allow me to remember, or actually learn, what I was seeing. Because they were distinct shapes and colors, those three countries stuck in my brain right away. This was encouraging. From there, we took on three more—Germany, France, and England. Three more colors; three more shapes. Wow! I had six now.

The rules were simple. We worked in groups of three and took a study break every 30-40 minutes. We never studied more than 40 minutes. The goal was to avoid cramming and fatigue and to build a reliable and accessible chain of information. I came to realize that if I followed Kevin's rules, I had more stamina. By creating many small study sessions rather than one large one, I was better able to retain and recall the information. I also came to see the breaks as little rewards. Kevin reminded me that all work and no play is tiring. The lesson was clear: Reward yourself for a good study session and build energy for the next one. I still do this today when I am memorizing large scores of music.

Reward yourself regularly. You deserve it.

Our breaks? Basketball. We shot hoops for 10 or 15 minutes and then got back to the map. Every once in a while Kevin would drill me while lined up for a free throw.

"What is the capital of Finland?"
"Ummm?"
"Upper right corner. The finger in green."
"Helsinki!"

It worked every single time.

The exciting part was that I didn't have to actually remember anything. All I had to do was see the map and for some reason my brain did that really well.

So test day came and I was as cool as can be. I was excited to try out my new skills. I wasn't frustrated or nervous because I had a cheat sheet. I could see the map in my head. This was an open book exam for me. I finished the test before anyone else, turned it in with a smile (which completely shocked my teacher), and got a perfect score. What a turn-around! This kid with an F just smoked his exam on European capitals like a child superstar genius.

My teacher phoned my parents.

"What's going on at home? I know he didn't cheat. There was no possible way to cheat but I have never seen anything like this." Furthermore, she was so impressed by the turn-around and excited that my cousin had figured out how to unlock the combination to the kid with no potential that she offered extra credit to help me pull up my grade. I ended that semester with a C in social studies even though, according to the math, I was far beyond saving. One test and extra credit should not have been enough to raise my grade. But my teacher understood more than just the math. Her job was to teach social studies but she saw that I had learned *how* to learn. She understood that this was a significant achievement and that I could apply this skill in all subjects moving forward. For these reasons, she allowed me to move on to the seventh grade. Once again, I was fortunate to have a teacher who saw the newly acquired potential in me; and that enabled her to bend the rules so that I would have a better chance at success.

This changed everything for me. Not that school suddenly became easy. No. Not at all. I would always struggle with test taking and translating dry or technical lectures into visual pictures. But now I knew that I was not dumb and, more importantly, I had the foundation of a system that I would continue to refine for many years to come:

1. Take Small Chunks
2. In Visual Layouts
3. 30 to 40 minutes a time

Thanks Kevin!

Some of the more progressive schools have done away with grades. They understand (as my social studies teacher did) that the math does not reflect the person. Grades don't necessarily help people realize their full potential; and isn't maximizing a person's full potential the whole point of an educational program? The focus should be on the person, remembering that every single person is *unique*. We are all unique, custom-made creations. That is why we are so valuable.

Exploration

> In contemporary society we have a tendency to blame others for anything that happens to us. It is much easier to play the victim than it is to "take the bull by the horns" and handle our own responsibilities.[4]

The years between the sixth grade and my senior year in high school seemed to pass very quickly and set me up for college and my professional life in ways that would shock me years later. When you focus on what matters most and are truly present in the moment, everything else seems to work out on its own. Things fall into place as if by magic. Don't get so caught up chasing your dreams that you forget to appreciate today. Today is all there really is. That is why it is called *the present*.

At the end of my sixth grade year, my mother received her first appointment with the United Methodist Church. She would have a two-point charge in the small town of Caldwell just outside of Milwaukee, Wisconsin. A two point-charge means that the minister serves two churches and the two churches pool their resources to create a full time job for the minister. Her two churches were the Caldwell United Methodist Church and the English Settlement United Methodist Church, where Tony Romo of the Dallas Cowboys grew up and went to church. My mom was their first female pastor. Fortunately, my father's job was mobile. As a claims adjuster he worked from an office in his home. So he stayed employed with American Family Insurance.

This was the first time I experienced packing and moving. It was exciting. Everything you owned had to be organized, packed up or thrown out. It was the ultimate in cleaning and starting

---

[4] *The Naked Voice: A Wholistic Approach to Singing* (2007). W. Stephen Smith and Michael Chipman. Oxford University Press.

fresh. This was an important skill to learn because I would continue to move every five years (or less) until I was in my 40s. If you include the amount of traveling I do for work this early experience in moving and learning a new community would become paramount to enjoying a healthy life on the road as a singer.

Singers can easily become ungrounded while traveling. Especially if they are in a foreign country and don't speak the language. Is it like being a traveling businessman? Sort of, except when I am under contract I might live in a particular city for many weeks at a time. I'm not on vacation and I'm away from home for many months. Having a skill set that keeps me grounded allows me to stay healthy physically and mentally. Because my contracts typically run between three and six weeks, having the ability to move often and easily has made living in new cities a joy.

The home we were moving to was large enough that my brother and I would have our own bedrooms for the first time. Our parents let us pick the colors we wanted for our rooms. I chose teal. Not light blue or a subtle shade of teal. I chose *teal*. It was bold and strong and I loved it. It's one of my favorite colors. In high school when my Dad and I built my 1965 Corvair together, the color I chose to paint the car was Corvette teal.

In school, I was the new kid for the first time in my life. That made me nervous. Anyone who has ever been the new kid knows that the first day of school can cause anxiety. Would I be the cool kid? The picked on kid? I fought less now but I still had a temper. Would the anxiety set me off and land me in the principal's office during the first week of school? I never had to ride a bus to school. Caldwell is a small town with a small handful of houses but walking to school (as I had done in Janesville) was not an option. This required me to stay on schedule when following my morning routine. The experience may be the reason that I can organize my time so well today. Previously, if I walked to school late I could still attend most of my classes. Now, if I missed the bus I missed the entire day.

This level of personal responsibility and time management became a very important skill set that continued to develop as I got older. It's easy to say that getting up for school on time was a requirement and not a skill, but this is when responsible time management started to take shape in my life. The result? Today, I can look at an opera score and calculate very accurately how long it will take me to learn and memorize the entire show. How much of this is nurture versus nature? It's hard to say. You can wake my father up in the middle of the night and he'll immediately tell you what time it is and what direction he is facing. It's a freaky skill and I've tested it. But I don't recommend waking up your parents too often in the middle of the night to perform experiments.

I didn't inherit my father's sense of direction. When I started driving, the family joke was that I could get lost in my own bathroom. However, my scrambled brain picked up some of my Dad's ability to calculate time. Never underestimate the value of your personal hands-on experiences. No matter how simple the task, that task is the foundation for what comes next. Every single day is a unique experience. Over time, all of those unique experiences add up to something extraordinary. And, yes, my sense of direction is much better today.

How was my new school? My fears were put to rest pretty quickly. All kids pick on each other as part of their social development, and I did have a couple of well-fought battles on the playground. But, all in all, I made some wonderful friends many of whom I am still in touch with today.

How was the music? Brilliant! It was one of the strongest choral programs in the area. Mrs. Hassey was in charge of the band and chorus for a couple of schools in the area and she was a force with which to be reckoned. Almost military in nature, she was terrifying and electrifying at the same time. She had to be. The typical classroom size in that area was anywhere from 16 to 30 students. There was only one class session for music and Mrs. Hassey had the largest class sizes in the school. Her large classes also indicated that her program was very popular and students loved working with her.

The major choral event of the year was the Spring Fling concert. This was an extremely popular production and the concert always packed the gym with families and members of the community. My singing skills hit Mrs. Hassey's ears the first day of class and she immediately set out to give me a solo in the Spring Fling. She wisely didn't *assign* a song to me. She introduced the song to me slowly so that I would not immediately write it off. What was the song? *People Will Say We're in Love* from Rogers and Hammerstein's musical "Oklahoma." I had never seen "Oklahoma," but I was cast as the leading man, Curly, in my high school production years later. Coincidence? Why did she think I would write it off? I was in the seventh grade. Love? Yuck! My first response was, "People will say I am not singing that song."

I remember being in the music room with a couple of friends when Mrs. Hassey told me that she had chosen a song for me. She announced the title in a strong voice and the room was filled with giddy laughter. I protested, saying that I wanted to sing *Mack the Knife.* How did she respond? She sat down at the piano and played *People Will Say We're in Love* to me. There was a huge smile on her face as she sang, making eye contact with me and raising her eyebrow as if to say, "See you like this don't you?" Actually, I did.

It was my first big solo in a concert situation but because of my Barbershop experience I wasn't nervous. However, I didn't know what to expect from the evening. The song fit my voice perfectly, and the audience roared when I finished. This was the first time I experienced applause like that. My friends were excited for me and from that moment on it was considered cool to be a singer. I felt like a star and my purpose gained more steam. Mrs. Hassey was honored as one of the top ten teachers in Wisconsin before she retired. We are still friends today.

During this time, my musical life outside of school was also about to expand in the arena of Barbershop music. While the solo bug had bitten me, I still loved the harmonies of Barbershop. We were far enough away from Janesville that my father had to resign as director of the Beloit chorus and we began looking for a new place to sing. There was a rather new chorus about an hour away from Milwaukee in Northbrook, Illinois that was making major strides in the competition scene. We decided to give it a try.

The New Tradition Chorus was directed by Jay Giallombardo, a fantastic musician, whose musical lessons continued to inspire me for many years. The chorus was different from my previous experience. It was a large chorus consisting of about 80 men and the expectations were at a professional level. They were perfectionists with intense rehearsals and I loved every minute of it. I responded positively to the concept of teamwork. I was still a kid and perfecting music was a hobby that I enjoyed. The enjoyment became part of a powerful lesson. This pursuit of perfectionism would later be tested when it came to paying my bills. Establishing a strong foundation based on singing well as its own reward helped me recover from a vocal breakdown early in my professional career.

Once again, I was treated like one of the guys. Being a member of this chorus also allowed my father and me to compete in our first International Barbershop Competition. It was held in San Antonio, Texas in 1988 and the chorus finished in fourth place. This was considered a very impressive finish for a new chorus in their first international appearance.

That very same contest would also be the year my biggest heroes in Barbershop would win the International Quartet Competition. Remember when I discussed mentors? The members of the *Chiefs of Staff* might be four of the all-time greatest mentors.

The Chiefs, as we called them, were the special guest performers on my very first Barbershop concert in Beloit and they were rock stars in my mind. Their music was exciting and their energy on stage was captivating. They didn't just sing songs, they told musical stories. I was immediately their number one fan. I never followed famous rock stars very much. For some reason a cappella music touched my soul and became my obsession. The Chiefs were famous to me and it was even cooler because I could meet them in person.

After the show, I bought their album on cassette tape. Remember the dishes? Each night after dinner I sang along with the Chiefs' album while I did the dishes. Within no time I learned the tenor part to every single song on their album and was well on my way to wearing out the tape. I didn't realize it then, because I was simply having fun, but the repetition of singing their brilliantly tuned harmonies over and over built powerful synapses in my brain. I was already training my ears, voice, and mind for a professional life in music.

Because I was such a fan of the Chiefs, my parents took me to see them perform in Madison, Wisconsin. After the late night show (or the afterglow as we called it), I asked the Chiefs if I could sing a song with them. This is where Barbershop mentors are so wonderful. Although they were rock stars in my mind, these were not full-time or even professional singers. They had *day jobs* in Illinois and sang in a really good a cappella quartet on the weekends. Which all adds up to say that when I asked if I could sing a song with them, they said yes. How often do you get to meet, let alone sing with, your heroes? How often does someone look up to us and we don't even know it?

Sam the Old Accordion Man. That was the song I wanted to sing. As soon as the song started, everyone in the room stopped talking and watched. When the song ended, the room erupted in massive applause. I found out later that even the Chiefs were blown away. They must have been thinking "Oh, neat! That little kid from the Beloit show wants to sing with us. How cute." But I could actually sing. They asked me to sing another song and asked which of their songs I knew. "All of them. I know all the songs on your album," was my answer.

This entire scene took place before we moved to Milwaukee. Often, events in life happen for reasons we don't connect with until years later. Our job is to enjoy the ride and appreciate the moment. What happened next could not have been planned if I had tried.

Once my dad and I were singing with Northbrook, we began attending the Illinois Barbershop contests. This was also the home District for the *The Chiefs of Staff*. They asked my parents if I could sing with them on the Friday night President's Show. It was to be a surprise cameo. They asked if I could sing the year before. My parents went to the fall convention in Illinois before we moved to the Milwaukee area and the Chiefs asked if I was with them. No. I was at home. Then, they asked if they could bus me from Janesville to Peoria, Illinois so that I could sing with them.

My parents felt that a solo bus trip of that nature was a bit much for a sixth grader so the invitation (which was a tremendous honor) would have to wait. It was well worth that wait. In fact, I think the Chiefs were more excited than I was. I was a kid and had no idea what singing on the President's Show meant. It's one of the biggest honors they could offer me. Today, it's one of my fondest memories.

The show took place in a huge ballroom at the convention center, which allowed audience members to sit at tables eating and drinking. It was a beautiful and energetic cabaret setting. The Chiefs made sure I was sitting at the front table. After a couple of songs, their tenor said he needed a drink of water and left the stage. As he made his exit, he handed me his jacket and I slowly put it on. Obviously, it was much too large for me. While one of the members was doing his MC work, the remaining two members started chatting and looking at me. They were setting up a funny scene and before you knew it they were motioning for me to come on stage, acting as if this was all unrehearsed and spontaneous.

The audience responded: "How cute! The Chiefs are going to sing with this kid." Then, we sang my favorite tune *Sam the Old Accordion Man*. The audience stood and applauded wildly. I honestly didn't know what to think or even what to do. My heart was beating harder during the applause than during the song and the noise from the crowd was so loud that my ears felt like they were going to burst. You might think that I would have basked in the moment taking in the exhilarating experience. But I was only 12 years old and was so blown away I didn't have a response. I was basically in shock! My parents made sure to explain to me that most of the people in the audience would never get to do what I had just done and might even be jealous. I would need to be humble and kind to every single person.

During this time, the Chiefs won their second bronze medal in the International Competition and as their tenor came back on stage he put one of their medals around my neck. With friends like that creating my musical foundation how could I not be inspired to continue in music? Tim McShane, Chuck Sisson, Don Bagley, and Dick Kingdon. Regular guys who you have never heard about and four of the most powerful mentors I ever had the pleasure of knowing.

How often do we underestimate the impact we have on someone? While the details of this story might seem like a fairytale, the essence of the story offers a simple lesson. It is a story of friendship. Friendships are powerful. They can make life-altering experiences every single day. Offering a hand in friendship does not require a certification, any level of education, and you don't have to be an expert at anything. A friend is someone who reminds you of your purpose when you've forgotten it yourself.

Living your Dream

From my journal—October, 27, 2011.

> Embrace all experiences in life and they will feed you. Avoidance, fear, and separation create anxiety. Anxiety leads to issues of control and a need to control leads to loneliness. The hard work should not always be "hard." A mountain lake is fed by many powerful mountain streams. Everyone and every experience is a mountain stream. Embrace them and you will celebrate life like the mountain lake.

The summer before my sophomore year in high school, mom was moved to a new church in Madison. The local arts and music scene was very active and Madison West High School provided the boost I needed to prepare for college. It was during my high school period, however, that my parents filed for divorce. The split was devastating and changed our family dynamic permanently.

The move to a larger city and college town was exciting. Living in the country was never the right fit and I enjoyed the activity of the city. There was always something to do, people to meet, and shows to see. At the time, Madison West High boasted the most number of National Society of High School Scholars students in the state. The school provided a high level educational program with college level offerings designed to prepare students for a professional future. That professional future included theatre and music.

To illustrate just how exciting the theatre department was at my high school, two of my classmates were Marc Webb, the director of *The Amazing Spiderman* movies and Sarayu Rao best known for her role as Angela on the Fox sitcom *Sons of Tucson* as well as playing Dr. Sydney Napur who appeared on David E. Kelley's *Monday Mornings on TNT*. The three of us are certainly not the only professional artists to graduate from Rebecca's program.

Who is Rebecca? Rebecca was the head of the theatre department and she was not to be called, *Ms.* anything. She was Rebecca, a large woman with an enormous heart and a massive passion for the theatre. She had a blazing speaking voice that could stop traffic without a megaphone. Her classes always went quickly for me because I am a visual learner who thrives in a hands-on environment. Rebecca's class was not about watching. It was about performing, and I loved to perform. This was not a class for those looking for an easy A. Rebecca had very high standards and developed some outstanding actors and theatre professionals in her time at West.

The highlight of the theatre year for me was the annual musical. Each year, Madison West staged one major student-performed musical—complete with orchestra. It was an impressive program. During my senior year, the musical was *Oklahoma*. I was cast in the leading role of Curly and both the girl who played Laurey and I would go on to become professional singers. In fact, more than ten people from that cast became professional artists. As you can imagine, with talent and potential like that on tap we put on one heck of a show.

Initially, I had a scheduling conflict with *Oklahoma* and was weighing whether or not I should audition. I had not been offered a leading role in a musical before, and didn't want to commit if I wasn't going to be available. I was not aware that wise Rebecca picked her shows based on the available talent. After I graduated, I learned that my inquiries into whether or not I should audition caused Rebecca to lose sleep. Knowing that she couldn't promise me anything before the audition, she finally said "Look you're the best singer in the school. What does that tell you?"

The musical ran two weekends with a total of four performances. There was a cast party after every show. Then, we received the biggest honor of all. Rebecca received an invitation to bring *Oklahoma* to The Wisconsin High School Theater Festival. This was a huge honor and very exciting. The challenge was securing the availability of the entire cast and Rebecca was apprehensive about the chances. To our amazement, everyone was available and anxious to take the show to the convention. We traveled with set, cast, orchestra, and crew to La Crosse, Wisconsin where we set up, rehearsed, and performed for high school students from all over the state. They were the best audience you could ask for and made us feel like rock stars. At the convention the following year, after I had gone off to college, *Oklahoma* was given special recognition for our performance at the Festival.

Each year my high school had a Theatre Awards Banquet and *Oklahoma* gave me the opportunity to win an award. During the show, Curly and Jud get into a fight over a girl. Curly goes to see Jud at his cabin and declares his romantic intentions for Laurey. Jud isn't particularly thrilled about this so Curly changes the focus by imagining aloud how people might mourn Jud's death by singing *Poor Jud is Dead*. Jud explains that if he is wronged, he is not opposed to repeating history and refers to a family whose house was burned down killing the entire family. As the tension rises Jud fires a warning gunshot into the ceiling. Curly coolly proves his own marksmanship by shooting out a knothole in the cabin wall.

This is a powerful scene—if the guns fire.

Our guns were basically cheap cap guns and were not always reliable. Sometimes when they fired a handful of caps went off sending black char across the top of my hand. Other times the guns would not fire at all.

One of the stagehands finally figured out (right before the show opened) that when a gun didn't fire his backup plan always worked. This was simply to roll the chamber half way around and pull the trigger again. So I was sent on stage with instructions that should my gun not fire, just turn the chamber half-way around and fire again.

Our scene was on. Jud pulled his gun out and fired at the ceiling. Bang! I slowly made a cocky quip about my shooting skills, lined up my gun, closed one eye and heard click. Click. Click. The gun would have to work or this scene just died. I replied with, "Just give me a second," and the audience laughed.

I rolled the chamber half way, pointed the gun back at the wall and heard, BANG! The audience broke out in applause as I blew the pretend smoke from my barrel, very western style. I gave Jud a knowing smile and he flexed every muscle in his face trying not to break character and smile back.

"Just give me a second," bang! That quip won me "Best Improvisation" of the year.

You might think with singing skills like mine that the chorus would have been a major part of my school day. Unfortunately (much to the frustration of the choir director), I didn't have time in my day for choir because I was involved in the theatre and Barbershop. However, I did make time for the band, and Mr. Rafoth was the one who introduced me to classical music.

When I arrived at West my sophomore year, I was an awful trumpet player. On a scale of one to worse I ranked in negative numbers. My tone was unfocused, I had no range, and my sense of rhythm was undisciplined. I was so bad that Mr. Rafoth later admitted that if he had known I would be his first chair trumpet player my senior year he might have quit teaching after my junior year. But he was also confused by my playing because he knew that I could sing. This realization is when everything started to change. One day during a particularly bad coaching session, Mr. Rafoth asked me to sing my trumpet line.

"You want me to sing?"
"Yes. You are a good singer aren't you?"
"Yeah, I guess. But sing with no words?"

"Yes. Just sing 'la la la.' "

I had no idea what he was getting at and was embarrassed to sing my trumpet part. As such my first attempt at singing "la la la" was quite half-hearted. He asked me to sing it again with more gusto. So I did, and he got excited. He said my singing was great and was exactly the kind of music making he was looking for in my trumpet part. Then he told me to play the trumpet just as I sang it. Game changer. Between connecting my voice to my trumpet and getting private lessons, I earned the first chair position in the Honor Band my senior year.

We often focus on what we do wrong. Take what you do well and use it to expand your skill set. It might take a little imagination to see how one skill enhances another but this process is much more powerful than focusing on what you do wrong and trying to *fix* it. People do not need to be *fixed*. We simply need to develop what we are already good at, no matter how simple the task.

As a school that supported the arts, West celebrated Fine Arts Week. This was a one-week event every school year that focused on the arts and gave students numerous opportunities to perform or host exhibitions. Events and performances were held all week and students could obtain a certain number of tickets to these events allowing them to skip class and enjoy a performance or exhibit. Because I sang, played the trumpet, was now taking piano lessons, and was in the theatre department, I scheduled something like 25 performances during Fine Arts Week my senior year and did not attend a single class. It was great.

Each morning before school I organized the day ahead. Each performance required a certain outfit, music, props, and so forth. I enjoyed Fine Arts Week so much that my scrambled brain did not forget a single detail, and I arrived early and well prepared to every performance. When you are doing what you love it never feels like work and this was certainly a labor of love.

My energy and performance record did not go unnoticed by the school administration. The year after I graduated, Rebecca told me the school instituted a *"Keith Harris"* policy limiting the number of performances a student can give. Maybe I should have attended just one class?

Now old enough to join my father and me in Barbershop, my brother also started singing. The three of us, along with a family friend, created the quartet *Family Ties*. The three Harris boys sang the top three parts; I sang lead and my brother was a full voice tenor. His voice had not changed yet. Family members often have similar voices and this is a great advantage when it comes to a cappella music. Because of the natural genetic blend, the quartet sounded good right from the start, and the fact that three of us lived together made rehearsing easy. As such, we made fast progress. The experience from singing in the Northbrook Chorus paid off, and soon *Family Ties* was preparing for the fall Barbershop contest in La Crosse.

Convention weekends are exciting and the Land O' Lakes District is very large which means events are well attended. At ages 12 and 16, my brother and I were the youngest competitors in the contest. We picked up many fans right away. Every quartet in the contest sings two songs on Friday night. Then, the top ten scoring quartets sing two more songs on Saturday night. My father and I had already competed together in the quartet *Ovation* so we knew the routine. But this was my first time singing lead, the very first district contest for my brother, and our fourth member had not sung in a quartet in years. For all practical purposes, we were novices.

Being that we were a new quartet, we didn't have any paid performances under our belt. We didn't have a lot of money. As a result, we stayed in one of the cheapest hotels in La Crosse. The owners worked the desk themselves. It was clean but it was dated and we had to drive a distance each day to the contest site.

You never know exactly how well the other competitors will prepare but I had high hopes we could finish in the top three.

Round one went well, and our name was announced to sing in the top ten. Round two went even better and created a real buzz with the audience. People started telling us that we were in first place or that they had us picked to win. I got my hopes up in previous competitions only to be disappointed, so I took the compliments to mean we had a strong future. You don't know who the winner will be until the announcements are made because the scoring is kept private. The winners are announced immediately following the competition.

Announcement time is always harder for me than the performance. I hate waiting and the announcers always seem to enjoy the drama of dragging out the awards ceremony. They announced third place, then second place and our name had not been announced. Maybe we were not in the top three as I had hoped?

"And your 1991 Land O' Lakes District Quartet Champion is..."

I was looking at the floor and started to get sick to my stomach.

"...Family Ties!"

I leaped out of my chair and jumped so high I could have dunked a basketball. My head was spinning; my ears were filled with the sound of cheering. By the time I caught my breath and headed to the stage to collect the trophy I realized the entire auditorium was on their feet and enjoying the reactions of all four of us.

This was such a wild and unexpected win that performance offers were handed to us immediately after we came off the stage. Most of them were hand written and one was written on a napkin. *Family Ties* went on to sing approximately 100 performances in our four years together. And what about that outdated hotel? By the time we got back it was about four in the morning. The owners had changed the sign out front to say "Family Ties! Yo!" What a great surprise to end the night! I highly doubt the swanky name brand hotels downtown would have done the same.

All in all, this chapter paints a pretty amazing picture doesn't it? It *was* amazing and I was enjoying school and the quartet very much. This was all about to change very quickly. Shortly after the big win with *Family Ties* my brother happened into my mom's office at the church right at the moment when she said to my father "I want a divorce."

Obviously, this was not how my parents intended to share the news with their children. My brother freaked out. He ran back to the house before my parents could collect themselves. I was at my desk doing homework. My brother ran into the room crying and told me our parents were getting a divorce. My first response was anger. I viciously attacked my brother and told him that he was being stupid and that he didn't know what he was talking about. He insisted that he heard it and the only form of support I could muster was to tell him to stop crying. In truth, my brother's news terrified me. A few moments later my parents came in and confirmed the news. Then both my brother and I were crying.

My feeling of being on solid ground evaporated in an instant. Many of my friends had divorced parents. Why was this so devastating? I saw how my friends split themselves between two homes and I always thought "At least I will never have to go through that. My family is secure." I truly believed that to be an unquestionable fact.

I have always been an optimist. It never occurred to me that ours would ever become a "broken home." That would never happen to *my* family. Those things only happen to *other* families. The divorce confused me. It was years since we had seen our parents argue. But the fighting hadn't stopped. They agreed to stop fighting in front of the kids. My brother and I simply didn't know the relationship continued to struggle. We thought everything was going quite well and were completely blind-sided by the news of a divorce.

All of this happened shortly before Christmas. Christmas has always been a magical time for me. I enjoy the mystery of the night, the Christmas Eve celebrations, and the late night services. Singing in the choir loft that Christmas Eve, I wondered if I was the only person in the church that night who was unhappy. The thought never occurred to me before. The experience opened my mind to the secret trials others carry every day.

My parents did their best to avoid putting the kids in the middle of their failed marriage. Nevertheless, I searched for answers, wondering if I could change the outcome. I wanted to fix things and return our life to normal. I spent years trying to understand why my parents divorced and why their stories were never in agreement. This event happened this way, and that event happened that way. I wanted a logical understanding. I *needed* a logical understanding. But all I came to understand is that my parents could not agree on anything. Their stories would never match and that is why they had to get a divorce. My sanity returned as I began to figure that out. That brought the understanding I was looking for and now I have developed separate relationships with each of them.

> Ask yourself a question: Would I rather understand
> my problems or just be free of them? If you would
> rather be free, I highly recommend letting go of
> wanting to figure them out.[5]

The very next day the first person I shared this news with was Rebecca. She let me cry on her shoulder and asked if my brother and I were close. "Sort of," I replied. She told me that in the end my brother and I would be very close. She didn't tell me to take care of him or that I would need him. It was as if a wise sage sent a blessing to my family. She was right. After a lot of language I won't print here, my brother and I are close. I would like to tell

[5] *The Sedona Method: Your Key to Lasting Happiness, Success, Peace and Emotional Well-being* (2003). Hale Dwoskin and Jack Canfield. Sedona Press.

you that we wear our scars with pride, but the truth is that some pains are always present. What changes is your life around that pain.

Think of a circle. If your life grows like a tree then you get a new ring every year. Your pain shows up on one ring. That ring may or may not heal but you keep growing new rings making the overall percentage of that painful ring less over time. Your new rings represent new experiences, relationships, and perspectives on life. This can even make the pain useful when developing meaningful relationships. Don't be in a hurry to bury or even heal your pain. That scar on your ring of growth is valuable.

The divorce announcement came shortly after the big win for *Family Ties*. This exhilarating win in combination with the announcement of my parent's divorce brought new meaning to the axiom "The show must go on."

Family Ties booked 20 more weekend engagements out of town that year. Performing in the midst of a family breakdown is beyond words. I'm not sure how my brother and I kept singing. Tensions were high and fights were common. During one performance, three of us got so heated that we began yelling at each other behind the curtain just before our name was announced. We were yelling one moment and smiling at the audience the next. It was a true Pagliacci experience. Other performers backstage must have thought we were crazy.

Should we have cancelled our performances and taken a break? For some reason it never occurred to any of us that we should cancel a few concerts. Would that have made a difference? I doubt it. You only win that big contest once in the Barbershop contest system, and when preparation meets opportunity you have success. This was a once in a lifetime opportunity and we wanted to make the most of it. So it was homework on the road, shows each weekend, and an exhaustive emotional mountain to climb.

And climb it we did—one step at a time. Because my brother decided to live with my father and I stayed with my mother so that I could finish high school, the quartet became the glue that kept my brother and me seeing each other every week. Carrying an emotional weight is a little like exercise. The first time you pick up a weight in the gym it feels pretty heavy. But over time if you continue picking up that same weight each day, it starts to feel lighter. The gym equipment has not changed. You've become stronger.

Life's adventures are only possible because of life's challenges.[6]

[6] *The Top Ten Things Dead People Want to Tell YOU*. Mike Dooley. ©Mike Dooley, www.tut.com

Chuck Sisson, Keith Harris, Don Bagley, Dick Kingdon during the President's Show, Peoria, IL, 1987.

Keith Harris and Tim McShane during the President's Show, Peoria, IL, 1987.

Keith Harris and Rebecca Jallings during Pippin,
Madison, WI, 1990.

Keith Harris, John Lowell, Paul Harris, Roger Harris ~
Family Ties, 1991.

John Rafoth and Keith Harris after Falstaff at
Lawrence University, Appleton, WI, 1996.

Kenneth Bozeman, Keith Harris, Joanne Bozeman,
Graduation from Lawrence University, Appleton,
WI, 1998.

Votre toast
Carmen
BIZET
1970s?

Julian Patrick, circa 1970.

Julian Patrick, 2004.

Keith Harris as the Barber in Il barbiere di Siviglia, Seattle,
WA, 2006.

Risk versus Reward

At this point in the story I am sure it's not going to shock anyone that I never did become the greatest test taker. Most tests aren't as easy as picturing a map. I was a hard worker, which meant my homework was spot on and by high school I was getting good grades. Unfortunately, homework assignments aren't a part of the ACT (American College Test). What a bad idea right? Let's have a visual learner with dyslexia and test anxiety sit in a room for eight hours and let's use that to determine if he belongs in college. Obviously, that didn't go well for me. My mom suggested I get a tutor and take the test again. Honestly I thought the entire concept was ridiculous, so I dismissed it without a second thought.

My mom asked "How will you get into college?" I replied "I can sing. If they don't like my singing I don't want to go to school there." Then I added "Plus, I have good grades so what kind of morons really put that much weight on a single test?"

To me, this was a completely logical statement. I didn't realize at the time how risky that statement was, and how close I came to a rejection letter. Furthermore, as if that didn't scare my mother enough, I only applied to one college. It was not the safe junior college fallback option either. I applied to a private college with one of the best music conservatories in the Midwest— Lawrence University in Appleton, Wisconsin.

Not only was I accepted to my college of choice but I was given a scholarship in vocal performance as well. My voice teacher and mentor for the next five years was Kenneth Bozeman. Ken was tall and thin with a beautiful tenor voice and he had a full head of dark hair—until I became his student. By the time I graduated, Ken sported a full head of silver hair.

And while it is helpful to understand the physiological and acoustical aspects of singing, those aspects alone are limited in their scope. Good technique must deal with the whole human organism.[7]

This statement illustrates exactly why Ken is such a powerful teacher. A good voice teacher knows technique but a great teacher understands the entire person. The voice is the sound of the human condition. It's the noise we make when we are surprised or the immediate cry released when we touch a hot pan and burn ourselves. Connecting this very personal and visceral part of the human expression to a structured training can be tedious. A teacher has to be part counselor and part mentor. Ken encompasses the best of both and during my five years at Lawrence we often talked as much as we sang. That is still true today.

Lessons at Lawrence generally ran twice a week for 30 minutes. As I grew and my skills expanded, half an hour wasn't always enough. So Ken would often schedule my lessons around the time of his lunch break or at the end of the day when he could give me extra time when needed. In preparation for my junior recital, we spent many of my lessons on his sun porch practicing German. Ken won a Fulbright Scholarship to study in Germany when he was younger. His German was excellent. Those lessons consisted of Ken speaking and me repeating the new sounds over and over until they became familiar and I was able to reproduce them without great effort.

Ken is a very gentle and consistent teacher. It's not that he is afraid to push his students. Rather, he does it with a loving hand. Although there was this one lesson during my senior year. After repeating a passage incorrectly many times, Ken slammed the piano lid down and yelled "No! You're a better musician than that."

---

[7] *The Naked Voice: A Wholistic Approach to Singing.* W. Stephen Smith and Michael Chipman.

Best lesson ever. Ken is also a master at tough love.

I've already mentioned that I learned early on that time is my friend and that I was given as much time as any millionaire or famous singer. I took on Lawrence with a vicious work ethic. By the time I reached my junior year I was completely exhausted and began to suffer from serious colds and bronchial infections. Clearly, something had to change. I needed to take better care of my health. A big part of my exhaustion was my sleep schedule. I was averaging four to six hours of sleep a night and singing and studying during the hours I was awake. My body couldn't handle that amount of work with such little rest. I enjoyed learning, but taking music theory, music history, voice classes, and learning all those languages all at once took its toll on my brain and became detrimental to my health.

Although I don't recommend working yourself to the point of exhaustion, a vigorous work ethic does, at times, produce some benefits. Following a concert one evening with the Santa Fe Opera company, a lady from Venezuela approached me and asked,

"Hablas Español?"
"No, not very well." I answered.
"But you knew what I said," she smiled.

As it turns out she addressed me in Spanish because my Spanish songs were so understandable she thought I spoke the language. This compliment is every singer's dream.

Knowing my body could not withstand the current schedule anymore, I decided to sleep eight hours a night, every night. If my homework didn't get done—so be it. If I flunked my classes because I ran out of time, at least I was going to be physically healthy. In other words, I reached the end of my rope and needed to upgrade my flight plan in order to continue my journey.

I allocated some of my precious time to resting and getting a good night's sleep, and an amazing thing happened. I made the Dean's List for the first time in my life. Furthermore, I stayed on the Dean's List for the rest of my time at Lawrence. In fact, I missed graduating with honors by 0.1%.

My homework was getting done faster, my brain was retaining the material, and my voice felt amazing. A proper night's sleep was giving my body what it needed to work more efficiently. This efficiency paid off in every aspect of my educational and professional development.

Isn't it interesting that I didn't decide to take proper care of my body until it was broken by my schedule? We all love to pretend we are super human, or we assume that everyone else is stronger than we are. We are quick to believe that we are weak and just need to *try harder*. But trying harder in and of itself can be an empty pursuit. It's a lot like stepping on the gas pedal of a car that has run out of gas. If the engine won't run you can push the gas pedal to the floor but nothing is going to happen. Sometimes we need to take a step back and take a fresh look at an issue. I took time away from homework to rest. That may seem like an illogical solution. But, the result was that I ended up needing less time to study and what I learned was retained. The "illogical" exchange of time turned out to be the perfect solution.

Staying organized. College life was so different from high school that I was completely overwhelmed. In high school, I basically had the same schedule every day. In college I didn't. Some classes met three times a week, some met twice a week. Then there were the rehearsals and voice lessons. After a while, it became a confusing wash of information and my scrambled brain could not keep track of it all. That was just the class load. Living on my own meant that I had to get myself to meals and do my own laundry.

Ken Bozeman came to the rescue. In my second week of classes he asked,

"How's it going? How are you settling in?"

This very simple question opened a floodgate that quite likely saved me from flunking out of Lawrence my first term. I explained that I was overwhelmed and that I could never remember where to go or when to go there. This was in the days before iPhones (and the now forgotten Palm Pilots), and until this time I never needed to keep a calendar. Ken introduced me to the magic of the Excel spreadsheet.

Across the top of the spreadsheet we put the days of the week and along the sides the time of day listed in 30 minute increments. Next, I filled in my schedule and posted it over my desk. Now, my brain could relax. I had a road map for the week. I built in time for homework, practicing, and laundry. This seems simple right? It may even seem obvious to some. But learning to organize myself this way turned into a tidal wave of organization that served as a template for the future.

My business has grown significantly during the past ten years and people often ask me the same question. As a singer, teacher, choral conductor, church musician, voice-over and recording artist, jingle singer, and now author, how the heck do I have time for everything? The answer is simple. I organize my time extremely well. I am able to accurately estimate the time needed to complete a given task. This enables me to schedule a number of tasks back-to-back and still get eight hours of sleep at night. There may be bumps along the way but even baby steps move us forward. The important thing is to continue making progress.

When was the last time you asked someone "How's it going? How are you settling in?" A simple inquiry into someone's day can seriously change a person's life.

My five years at Lawrence earned me a double degree—Bachelor of Music in Choral Education and Vocal Performance. One of the requirements was to student-teach in the public school system. My assignment consisted of teaching classes from kindergarten to the twelfth grade. That experience ensured that I would never pursue a classroom of my own.

You recall earlier in this book that my third grade teacher wanted to move me to a reading group with kids that had intellectual and developmental disabilities. Those wounds run deep and my experience as a student teacher brought them back to the surface. My experience in the third grade happened in the early 1980s and I assumed that by the 1990s there had been substantial improvements made with respect to handling kids who were misunderstood as I had been. It made me sick to my stomach to find myself right back in the third grade again and recalling what it was like to be the dumb kid in class.

Early in my grade school teaching, I spotted a boy who was always silent. I assumed that this boy was considered the "weird kid." Knowing exactly how that feels, I managed to connect with him and was able to teach a productive and enjoyable class. After class, however, the teacher who ran the classroom told me that she was glad that particular boy behaved for me because he was a real handful and didn't belong in her classroom.

"What do you mean," I asked? She took out one of his assignments and said, "Look at his handwriting. He's a mess. I don't know what's wrong with his brain but the letters are backwards and his words are out of order. Who writes like that?"

Mustering up all of my courage, I said, "He's not dumb. He's dyslexic and so am I." The teacher paused for a moment, looked at me and then said, "Well, I am sorry for you but I don't know what that means and he doesn't belong in my classroom. I don't have the resources to deal with that so it just ends up being a pain in my ass."

There I was back in third grade again. The dumb kid. My face became flushed, my breath was short and I couldn't speak. It was absolutely unbelievable to me that a teacher (who should have known better) wanted to move this kid to a class with intellectual and developmental disabilities because she wasn't willing to educated herself as to how to overcome a more challenging situation. This was particularly frustrating because I had just demonstrated how it was possible to reach that bright young student.

I wish I could tell you that I went to the principal's office and changed education for the better. The truth is, I felt so defeated that I was in my car as soon as the final bell rang. Getting away from that school could not happen fast enough and I could not wait until my teaching assignment there was completed.

So often we are too quick to judge. Does judging make us feel better? Why do we assume our perspective is the best for everyone? That the way we learn or understand information is the best and the only correct version? Why is it so hard to simply ask a question and then listen for the answer? Really *listen* without prequalifying how we'll answer. Nature has provided us with two ears but only one mouth for good reason. Leaders and educators who understand and respect this balance will have a much more powerful impact on every person they meet.

"How's it going? How are you settling in?"

Keith Harris, Susan May, Russ May after *Carmina Burana* with the Savannah Philharmonic, GA, 2012.

Keith Harris at Avery Fisher Hall after Beethoven's Ninth Symphony with the National Chorale, NY, 2014.

Listen to Your Body

> The world within is the cause, the world without
> the effect; to change the effect you must change
> the cause.[8]

The exhaustion I overcame at Lawrence provided me with a method to track when a sickness started and take steps to improve my overall health. How did I do this? By listening to my body. I started slowly tracing the process backwards each time I came down with something. It allowed me to be more in-tune with my body and what it needs to maintain good health. Sure, I still get sick; but I am often able to avoid the debilitating and reoccurring bronchitis I suffered in college.

> Our physiology creates disease to give us feedback,
> to let us know we have an imbalanced perspective,
> or we're not being loving and grateful. So the
> body's signs and symptoms are not something
> terrible.[9]

I realized that a serious chest infection often began two weeks earlier at a time when I was exhausted. Rather than resting and letting my body catch up with itself, I burnt the candle at both ends until I was forced to rest by getting sick. No one likes to get sick. But for a singer an illness can be even more frustrating. We rely on our voices to make a living, and our audiences rely on us to give them a wonderful performance. When we are sick either the performance suffers or (when we have to cancel) our paycheck suffers. In either case, the situation is less than ideal.

---

[8] *The Master Key System & Your Invisible Power: Get Both Great Works In One Ultimate Self Help Collection* (2008). Charles Haanel and Genevieve Behrend. Simon and Schuster.
[9] *The Secret* (2006). Rhonda Byrne. Atria Books.

This is why professional singers keep in tune with their bodies so that they can track the earliest stages of an illness. They recognize the importance of catching it before it turns into something much larger. Listen to your body. It will tell you exactly what it needs.

I have been fortunate in that during the past 30 years I have only cancelled one performance (knock on wood). I have, however, been hung over.

One evening after a concert (when I was much younger), the company hosted a dinner for the artists and their host families. It was great fun, and I enjoyed meeting some very interesting people. I had to get up at 3:00 am the next morning to catch my van to the airport. Upon reflection, I should have left the party early and gone right to bed. I left with my host family around 10:00 pm. My host was a retired LAPD officer, approximately 72 years old, and he asked if I would enjoy a scotch with him before bed. Well, of course I would.

As the saying goes, one thing led to another and we talked for hours. We had many common interests and as we talked the glasses just kept being refilled. The next thing I knew it was 2:30 in the morning, the bottle of scotch was empty, and I was completely hammered.

Somehow I managed to pack my bag and was ready for my bus by 3:30. It was a shuttle van service that picked me up at the house. I don't remember much about the ride to the airport, but apparently I puked all over myself. At least that is what I was told by the police as I proceeded to check in for my flight. I am rather impressed that I actually found the United Airlines desk, as I have no memory of arriving at the airport.

I was so far gone that I didn't smell anything unusual and was oblivious to the fact that I had emptied my dinner and all that scotch down the front of my shirt. The conversation with the police went something like this.

"Sir, you have puked all over yourself."
"I have?"

"Ummm... yeah. Maybe you should go to the bathroom and clean up. You can't check in for your flight right now."

"Oh, wow! Okay, I'll do that."

It was only when I got to the bathroom that I realized I had showered myself in the most impressive mess I had ever seen. I was covered from head to toe in spaghetti and scotch. You don't want to know what that smells like. I am pretty sure I over paid for the bus too or maybe they took extra money for the cleaning. I don't remember. But when I checked my wallet I was missing $20. Based on my condition, only charging an extra $20 was very generous on the part of the bus company.

The police continued to check on me now and again as I ate breakfast and gradually found my way to a clearer head. Once they realized I was just an idiot and not a security risk they left me alone. To my amazement United Airlines took pity on me and rebooked my flight without charging me a change fee.

I was so embarrassed and ashamed by that experience that I fell into a deep depression the following week. As a result, I have never been drunk in a professional setting since that day. Today, however, I got a good chuckle out of writing and sharing the story. We all make mistakes now and again and sometimes, as in my case, we publically humiliate ourselves. The lesson was much less painful than the act, but my experience required the act in order to learn the life lesson. Don't be too quick to judge yourself. Be willing to look in the mirror and learn from the things you want to do differently next time.

For someone with a strong work ethic, balancing my day and taking care of my body is not always easy. But the body is your instrument case, so it is a good idea to treat it as if you're protecting a Stradivarius. Good health is founded in diet and exercise. I don't know if we can actually extend our lives by practicing good habits or whether length of life is set in our genes; but I do know that we can have a massive impact on the quality of that life through diet and exercise.

I was led to exercise through a car accident. As an active kid I was always involved in sports, and fitness was not something I thought about. In high school, however, I focused on theatre and music and stopped playing sports. The result was that I ended up about 30 pounds heavier than I am today. It was the car accident that provided me with a requirement to stay fit.

I was in the front passenger seat of the 1965 Corvair that my father and I built together. The night before, I attended the *Oklahoma* cast party and it was a very late night. I felt it would be more responsible for my friend to drive my car to a Barbershop event scheduled the next day. It was about a 45-minute drive and I didn't want to fall asleep at the wheel.

On our way home everything changed and it happened in a matter of seconds. My friend made a left hand turn but misjudged the oncoming traffic. The car was struck in the passenger front corner at about 30 miles per hour. The force was so strong that my shoulder dented the inside of the door and my hands crushed the passenger side dash panel. At the time of the damage, beyond the emotional crisis that my classic car had just been destroyed, there seemed to be a few stitches required in the back of my right arm.

The long-term damage was much more serious. The force of the accident combined with the fact that the car was only equipped with lap belts, resulted in a herniated disc at the bottom of my spine. Fortunately, the disc is healthy but the tendon that holds the disc in place is gone on the left side. The accident literally snapped it like a rubber band.

There were years of struggling with back pain before my back issues were finally properly diagnosed. The pain was caused by the herniated disc. The disc is the soft padding that keeps the vertebrae bones from touching each other. The tendons hold that padding in place. Because one of my tendons is missing, my disc squirts out like the jelly in a donut. When it is inflamed or enough force pushes on the disc the result is that it touches the nerves close by sending debilitating pain down my back and left leg. I already had a squishy mid-section to compliment my squishy disc, so my back flared up often.

The cure? Strengthen my core. I have to stay fit to stay pain free. It works better than painkillers. Because the basic structure of my body is missing a key component, I live a normal, pain-free life by increasing the muscle strength around the injury. Jumping into fitness was not easy. I started small and over time increased my workout routines, periodically taking on new challenges. Now, I am a graduate of the P90X, P90X2 and Insanity programs from Beach Body, and have run five Full Tough Mudder events, a 10 mile military grade obstacle course. The result is that I am much more comfortable traveling and can handle a long week of rehearsals on my feet. Getting fit not only helped me to sing better it increased my durability.

Well that's just great isn't it? If you're reading this book and you're still in the squishy mid-section stage of life, and don't have the motivation of pain to get you out and on the move, where do you start? Feeling better or getting fit is not about building a temple overnight; and it's certainly not about creating so much muscle pain you can't even get off the couch. Start easy. Go for a walk and work up a sweat. Go dancing. Do something active that is fun. Do it every day for two weeks and you'll be amazed at the way your body responds.

> Show up, every day, moving in the direction of your dream. Physically, to any degree you can, do something. These are the baby steps. They always seem futile. You may be dreaming of champagne and caviar, yet you have to ride the bus to your interview at the mall. Do it anyway. It doesn't matter that you aren't sure if you're on the right path; chances are you're not. Do it anyway. If you have absolutely no idea of which direction to move in, move in any direction.[10]

---

[10] *The Top Ten Things Dead People Want to Tell YOU*. Mike Dooley. ©Mike Dooley, www.tut.com

People often say to me, "Oh it must be so great to travel all the time." Yes. I am very fortunate to travel and sing in places I might have never visited on my own. But traveling is not always glamorous.

Let's start with flying. The airport offers a fascinating glimpse at a wide range of people from all walks of life. I prefer flying during the week because during the week you generally fly with experienced travelers. On the weekends and holidays you travel with everyone else. There isn't really a category for *everyone else* you just have to be extra patient with some travelers.

I have some basic rules for flying:

1. Always travel with earplugs. Not only does it help block the tiring white noise of the airplane, but it does a wonderful job of drowning out the screaming babies. Of course, the babies cannot help that their ears feel like they might explode due to the change in pressure but their voices are very impressive in an enclosed space.

2. Always travel with a book and get it out as soon as you get to your seat. Although I like meeting people, an airplane is not the best place to talk for hours on end when you're a singer. That dry air can be tiring on the voice.

3. Never sit next to the screaming baby. This is self-explanatory and comes from experience as I have seen innocent travelers get christened in baby puke.

4. Whenever possible travel with carry-on luggage. Not only is it convenient but if you have a concert or a meeting, lost luggage could have you arriving slightly underdressed.

Airlines are really packing people in these days. I understand the more people you get on a plane the more money you can make. But how the heck is a 6'5" 300 pound man supposed to fit in those tiny seats? Fortunately, I am only 5'11" and 170 pounds so basic economy works well for me. I do not, however, fit in half a seat. Airlines are simply not creating space for people who require more room. This means if you end up sitting next to a large person you get to cuddle.

I was flying back to Seattle (my home at the time) from a weekend of singing. As usual, I got to my aisle seat right away, put my earplugs in and grabbed a book. After almost everyone was seated, I noticed the seat next to me was empty. This was either great news or really bad news. Either the seat was not booked or the person booked in that seat was having some problems.

Then I saw her coming. It was like the world suddenly moved in slow motion. You know those moments when everything stops and your focus goes tunnel vision? I saw a person heading down the aisle towards me—a large, older, unhealthy looking woman. Somehow her hair even looked unhealthy and her entire demeanor told me she was having a really bad day. She came down the aisle, looked at the seat next to me, and said,

"SHIT! I told that jerk to give me an aisle seat. Like they ever listen to anything you say."

She beat her carry-on into a place (it really should not have been able to fit) and then announced that, in order to not bother me for the rest of the flight, she would go to the bathroom now. Upon returning, she spent a number of minutes trying to find the exact position that would keep her content for the next three hours. Of course, she was using all of her seat and half of mine.

During the flight my new friend took it upon herself to see what I was reading.

"Oh, you like opera," she asks?

I was reading a book about opera.

"Yes, I am an opera fan," I stated briefly.

"Do you go to the opera often," she continued?

"Yes. I suppose I do," not looking up from my book.

"Are you a singer?"

"Yes," focusing harder on my book. I could feel the next question coming.

"Are *you* an opera singer?"

For some reason it never occurred to me that I could just say no and continue sharing my book in silence.

"Yes," I replied

"OH WOW! Are you going to a performance or coming home from a performance?"

"Both."

"Do you sing with Seattle Opera?"

"Yes."

She then spent the next few minutes telling me about an opera she saw, and how much she hated it. She was the absolute expert. Then she continued by explaining how she had been a season ticket holder for the ballet but had not been to the opera in years. Of course, she wanted my name so she could watch for it. People always say they want to watch for my name. I wonder if anyone really ever remembers my name.

At this point we were deep enough into the conversation that I decided to invite her to see my next performance. This brought us full circle back to the conversation about the opera she didn't like, but she promised she would look into it. I am pretty sure she was busy that night.

One of the keys to staying grounded while on the road (beyond the need for a little patience) is to have a daily schedule. Rehearsals often run six hours a day in two three-hour segments, six days a week. If I am only on call for three hours one day, that leaves a lot of time to fill. This is where inexperienced travelers can get themselves into trouble. When you're alone in your hotel it is easy to become bored and lonely. This can lead to decisions you'll regret later. I find that by traveling with the things I enjoy, I am able to create a healthy structure, or a daily schedule for my life on the road. For example I enjoy:

1. Exercise;
2. Cooking;
3. Reading;
4. Watching movies; and
5. History and art of the local area.

The combination of taking an interest in the local community, along with having a daily schedule, keeps me busy and offers a feeling of accomplishment. While I think this lesson is valuable for anyone, this is absolutely vital if you're away from home often. It's true that even with structure not everything will go according to plan. There will still be local customs and surprises that will catch you off guard. For example, once while singing in France I learned about the local mosquito population the hard way.

I was singing at a festival on the island of Belle Isle just off the coast of Brittany in France. The weather was beautiful and, still jet lagged, I went to sleep around midnight to a gentle breeze from the window. A couple of hours later, I awoke to a buzzing noise in my ear. Mosquitoes. At first, it was just an annoyance. But then the problem became much more serious. Those little monsters were hungry and kept me awake for nearly three more hours. Assuming it was only a small handful of surprisingly aggressive mosquitoes, I didn't think to simply shut the window.

I am not exactly sure what made them stop, or if I just became exhausted enough to sleep through the feeding. At the time, it seemed the biggest annoyance was the buzzing around my head but the real punch line came in the morning when I went to the bathroom. You know those scenes in movies where you see someone heading to a mirror and the next shot is the outside of the house and all you hear is screaming? That was exactly how it went down when I saw my pizza face.

Those little monsters destroyed my face. Even better, I had a concert to sing that night. I had two choices—I could look like I broke out in hives, or I could wear make-up. I figured the lights would wash out most of the bites so I skipped the make-up and went with the hives.

The official count was 35 bites on my face and close to 100 bites on my entire body. Thank goodness I don't have any allergies and didn't become sick after the attack. I quickly learned the French word for mosquito, bought a plug-in repellent, and kept my windows closed after that.

Staying flexible in life requires both mental and physical discipline. Sometimes we learn the best discipline from our mistakes. I offer my stories as examples of how many different turns life can take. Your life takes just as many interesting turns. Too often, when they are our own personal stories, we don't think of them as interesting. Instead, we judge them as problems, issues, and hassles. We bury them, hoping no one ever sees how imperfect we are. Why are we insecure? What's wrong with being insecure? Will insecurity put you in the hospital? Does imperfection cause a physical pain you can't withstand? Insecurity and engaging in the school of hard knocks certainly comes with uncomfortable physical sensations. These sensations, however, are the key to our ultimate progress.

Listen to and feel those physical sensations without judgment. Don't be in a hurry to put a name on what you think you feel or to judge your personal experiences. Just be your own best friend and listen to your body. Nature is smart. Your body is constantly reaching out to you and teaching you something.

Mindset

> The reason, as with anything you do in life, is if you do not commit yourself fully to this process, you will not reach its full benefits.[11]

After graduating from Lawrence I moved away from the state of Wisconsin for the first time in my adult life; 2,000 miles away to Seattle, Washington. Clearly, teaching in the public school system was not my calling and because applying to one University had worked out so well the last time, I only applied to one graduate program. The University of Washington offered me a scholarship in vocal performance enabling me to get my Masters in Music.

The reason I chose the University of Washington (beyond the amazing scenery) was to study voice with Julian Patrick. By the time I met Julian, he was already 72 years old, enjoyed a well-traveled international operatic career as a baritone, and could still sing as if he was 40. A truly remarkable man, Julian's heart was as warm as his voice. His speaking voice sounded a lot like James Earl Jones, and his booming laugh was just as carefree.

Studying voice with a master who was 50 years older than me was both fascinating and frustrating. Julian forgot more music than I ever learned and while we made great progress while in Seattle, his vocal lessons made more sense to me years later. I still hear Julian's voice in my head today. It is as if Julian knew I wasn't ready for everything he could teach and planted lessons in my brain that would pop up and improve my singing years later. Now that Julian has passed, his urgency to get those messages across to me seems all the more pertinent.

---

[11] *The Naked Voice: A Wholistic Approach to Singing.* W. Stephen Smith and Michael Chipman.

Lawrence University is a liberal arts college focused on obtaining a well-rounded education. My Biology 101 class, for example, was the same Bio101 class for science majors. The master's program in Seattle was completely different. There, I was allowed and encouraged to focus on my specialty and I loved every minute of it. Up to that point, school always consisted of putting up with classes I had to take so that I could pursue the classes I wanted to take. In the master's program, I only took classes in my field of study and focused most of my time in the practice room figuring out my voice.

If you're a scientist or computer technician, the lab is your practice room. The lab is where you try out new skills, make mistakes, and master your processes. I loved the practice room and still think of my practice time as an experimental field for sound. As such, I believe growing professionals should always have a healthy dissatisfaction with the quality of their work. A healthy dissatisfaction means contentment with your work today and excitement to improve your product tomorrow.

It was at the University of Washington that I first sang the baritone solos for the *Carmina Burana*, a fantastic tour de force for the baritone. While it was arguably a bit of a stretch for me when I first sang it, this work has continued to push my vocal growth more than any other work and today is the most performed concert on my resume. This one work has taken me all over the United States and to every major concert hall in New York City including: Carnegie Hall, David Geffen Hall (previously Avery Fisher Hall), and Alice Tully Hall. This is also the work I was performing when the story that created this book finally surfaced.

It was very satisfying to start a new program with a fully developed set of study skills. Now I knew how to work with dyslexia, my test taking had improved, and I had developed a process to memorize music quickly. I think I could have graduated with a 4.0 grade point average and it was empowering to know that I could choose where to focus my time. Graduating with only a 3.8 felt easy after so many years of struggling in school.

In the American operatic system the best transition for singers from school to career is through the Young Artist Programs. These programs offer singers a chance to perform as an apprentice artist, coach with the top teachers in the world, and hopefully bridge the gap between school and career. After completing my two-year program at the University of Washington, I was accepted into three of the top apprentice programs in the United States: Santa Fe Opera, Seattle Opera, and Opera Theater of St. Louis. These programs offered a mountain of opportunities. As such, the transition from school to apprentice was quite easy. The transition from apprentice to professional was much harder and is where many singers quit.

Being a freelance singer is quite literally building a business and, as anyone involved in sales or freelance work knows, this is not an easy or overnight process. Because the only product on the shelf is your voice and one cannot rush the speed of the body's maturation process, developing this one product can take many years. Often, the male voice does not fully mature until the mid-40s which means in order to succeed a singer requires an attitude of all or nothing. If you have a backup option chances are you'll take it because the road to self-employed artist is simply too difficult and there are no guarantees. Young Artist Programs offer singers a glimpse at the life of a singer while making just enough money to survive.

Pursuing your dreams is difficult because unique people are the ones who pursue extraordinary ideas. Unique is not something with which we are comfortable. Unique is often mistaken for weird. It makes us uncomfortable to be weird so we suppress what makes us unique. As a kid, they made fun of me for being weird and my response was to fight. When that didn't work I tried to become the people pleaser, the good student, and sought approval, which was an empty pursuit. No one likes being ridiculed because it hurts. What do we do instead? We act like someone we think we should be, pretending to be someone we are not. We seek approval because of our insecurity, or we abandon our dreams all together. We make safe, logical decisions rather than weird passionate life choices.

If you miss the boat, work hard to catch up.[12]

If you look closely at successful people there is something weird about them that makes them stick out and makes you remember who they are. What is the key to success? Celebrate and become friendly with your unique weirdness. Once you accept what makes you unique, and you truly express and focus that uniqueness into your work every day, dreams are yours for the choosing. Don't misunderstand me. It takes a lot of effort to be true to your inner self. Don't expect special attention. Accepting what makes you unique does not mean society should cater to you. Your uniqueness is your gift, your purpose, and you are the only one who can develop that into something extraordinary.

Life will challenge us in frustrating ways as if to ask "How bad do you want this?"

There will be times you decide you don't want it, and you will see the challenges as powerful guides to a new path. Other times—even in the strangest of situations—your challenges strengthen your mission.

While on tour with the Santa Fe Opera we performed in Los Alamos. I am not sure exactly why but the stage manager arrived at the theater only 30 minutes before our performance and she was in no mood for chitchat. She introduced herself to us by complaining that we were already in the theater and was shocked that audience members were already coming in. You did read that correctly. We were having this conversation 30 minutes before the performance.

The story gets even better from here. Often, theaters protect their beautiful grand pianos by locking them and this theater was no different. What made this theater different from others is that

---

[12] *Inside Steve's Brain* (2008). Leander Kahney. Portfolio Publisher.

the key to the piano was not kept in the building. Our friendly stage manager didn't have a key for the piano. The only key was 45 minutes away and supposedly was en route.

After waiting 30 minutes past the show's starting time, and knowing that many audience members had been in the house for an hour, we decided to check out the old upright piano that was backstage. Now, I am not making any general statements about upright pianos, just this one. It was worse than a saloon piano.

How badly did we want to perform? With an audience already sitting in their seats should we give up and embarrass the theater by announcing a cancelled performance? Or, could we use this saloon piano to give people a lively show? How weird were we willing to be? We chose to perform and while not under the conditions we had hoped, moved our audience to a standing ovation.

The key finally showed up as we were walking offstage. Our pianist asked "Did you know we would need the piano today?"

"Yes," the gentleman answered. "I had it tuned last week for you and I had the same problem last week."

People and events sometimes seem to block progress just for the sake of being difficult. Sometimes life feels like a football game and whoever has the ball, or is being successful, will find him or herself the most blocked, tackled, and challenged. We can focus our attention on the roadblocks or we can create new roads.

A friend of mine arrived to a rehearsal late and a little tussled.

He said to me in a huff "You know when you're driving and you hit every red light and every single slow person is in the left hand lane?" "Oh yeah," I replied. He looked at me and smiled. "That's not why I am late. I am just late."

Celebrate your own uniqueness when things are going well and when you're just late.

Keith Harris as Valentin in Faust, Annapolis, MD, 2016.

Keith Harris as Papageno in Die Fauterflöte,
St. Petersburg, FL, 2018.

Loss

> I suspect that those who never succeed in
> analyzing their technique are the ones with short
> careers, because vocal problems come to all
> professional opera singers eventually.[13]

In December of 2002, I won one of the biggest competitions of my life, the Seattle Regional Metropolitan Opera Auditions. The honor took me to New York City to compete in the Metropolitan Opera house with 20 other singers from the United States. Some are still good friends and colleagues. Winning a contest is something most singers do not get to experience, and it isn't something on which any singer should depend. I had already booked a spring break vacation with my brother to Mexico during the finals in New York. Maybe, making other plans took the pressure off and was just the push I needed to secure the top position that day. I still haven't taken that spring break in Mexico.

> From my journal—September 9, 2002.
> > I believe so much in what I am doing that I know I
> > need to keep going. Although it does take a bit of
> > luck to really "make it," I am meeting some neat
> > people who believe in me and with that, maybe I
> > can create some of my own luck.

The Seattle Region of the Metropolitan Opera Auditions is one of the most funded in the nation and their prize money is very impressive. On top of that, a donor, moved by my performance, sent me a check for $1,500 to assist in my continued growth.

During the Metropolitan Opera competition, all of the singers were given a tour of the building. The Metropolitan Opera house is an impressive structure. It's easy to get lost and I would not be

---

[13] *Great Singers on Great Singing: A Famous Opera Star Interviews 40 Famous Opera Singers on the Technique of Singing* (2004). Jerome Hines. Limelight.

surprised if there were singers who have never found their way out. During our tour we were taken to a room where the details of the week were laid out for us. Early on in that talk the speaker said, "90% of you in this room will have a singing career." The statistics showed that if you made it to this point in this competition, you were in the thin air.

As if on cue, we looked around the room at each other wondering which of us were among the 10%. I went on to make my Metropolitan Opera debut seven years later. But the road to getting there was interrupted by a complete personal and vocal breakdown.

It seemed that after the win at the Metropolitan Opera Auditions and with a summer lined up with Opera Theater of St. Louis I was on a roll. Immediately following the Metropolitan Opera auditions, however, my body started changing. Up to that point I was considered to be a light baritone; some people thought I might be a tenor. Apparently, I had not finished maturing. In the months that followed, my chest grew, my voice deepened, and everything changed. I didn't know how to use my voice. The voice I was used to was gone and this new instrument didn't function in the same way. Because I was away from Seattle for the summer, I didn't have a voice teacher to help me through the transition.

The physical change was only part of my dive into the vocal abyss. That spring I met a girl. Our relationship intensified very quickly and before I knew it we were planning a wedding. We were married after only one year of dating. I had doubts before we got married but by the time the planning started I didn't know how to get out of the relationship.

My wife to be was an emotional handful and after we were married she became physically and emotionally abusive. All my time and attention were focused on trying to make her happy. My vocal studies suffered, I lost my purpose, and my spirit faded. I even looked physically ill. Friends and family later told me that my eyes looked so dark they thought I was hiding a serious illness. I was ill but it wasn't something a doctor could cure.

> Do not let the behavior of others destroy your inner peace. ~ Dalai Lama.

The voice represents the sound of the spirit and my spirit was crushed. My voice became weak and unreliable. It responded like a light with a bad electrical connection. One moment everything seemed okay and the next there was no sound or the sound was unhealthy. Knowing the voice was no longer reliable I stepped away from the opera business. I knew that singing badly at back-to-back auditions could be harmful to my career, so I found a job in a church choir. This musical connection kept me going while I figured out how to survive my marriage.

> Resistance prevents us from moving ahead in all areas of our life, especially in the area of personal growth and happiness.[14]

They say that just before a plane breaks the sound barrier the cockpit shakes the most. The longer we were together the more violent were my wife's outbursts. I was conflicted. I knew this was not a healthy relationship, but I made a commitment to be with this person in sickness and in health. Abuse is a sickness, right? So I should see it through. Eventually, I had nothing left to give.

I was not planning to leave the night I left. I simply had no reason to stay. After one of the most violent attacks, my wife headed to the bathroom to take a bath. I stood in the living room completely shell shocked. I was done. I grabbed the keys to my car, left the apartment, and never looked back.

> Dwelling upon what once hurt you will only bring new surprises, new losses, more disappointments—new reasons to be hurt.[15]

---

[14] *The Sedona Method: Your Key to Lasting Happiness, Success, Peace and Emotional Well-being.* Hale Dwoskin and Jack Canfield.

I spent the next two months living in hotels and sleeping ten hours a night. I had to physically recover before moving to New York City. My friends were there when I needed them. My wife wanted complete control over me and had gradually broken off communication with them. When I left, she was working on doing the same with my family. Leaving my marriage was like walking out of a dark cave and I am gratified to say that my friends were at the mouth of the cave waiting for me. Most of them told me "We knew you'd be back."

My vocal recovery started with Mark Oswald, a gentle soul who helped re-ignite my spirit and bring back my voice. It continued with Patricia Mccafffrey, a true voice whisperer, who studied with Julian Patrick's voice teacher. It really is a small world.

I don't wish an abusive relationship on anyone and I certainly don't ever want to relive that experience. But this horrid three-year relationship made me a better singer and a better person. During the divorce my ex-wife's lawyer was brilliant at stopping progress and making sure I had nothing but the clothes on my back for as long as possible. Ultimately, I was allowed to reclaim my personal belongings and even some furniture. Nine months later, when I retrieved my stuff, I no longer needed those items. Not because I could afford to replace them. Not at all. I had no money. Once I was allowed access to my belongings I appreciated having a couch but my personal attachment had changed. Living with nothing provided a powerful lesson. Of course, I wish I had the box of WWII memorabilia from my grandfather that my ex-wife tossed in the trash. But she could not take away the memories of my grandfather and the times I spent playing his trumpet. When everything else is stripped away you learn what is truly valuable.

---

[15] *The Top Ten Things Dead People Want to Tell YOU*. Mike Dooley. ©Mike Dooley, www.tut.com

The same happened with my voice. At my lowest point there were times that I could not sing at all, and when I was able to sing it wasn't good. This taught me that my voice is a precious gift that can be taken away at any moment. I enjoy every single day now that I can sing. Even on days when I am not feeling well or my voice cracks I still think "Yeah, but at least I can make sound."

My appreciation for my voice grew in immeasurable ways when it was taken away. Ken Bozeman was the first mentor in my circle to have the courage to guide my vocal recovery. I wanted to believe that my voice wasn't as bad as I feared so I sent Ken a recording for his review. This is risky when you're emotionally drained because singers never want to hear that they are a complete mess. Sending the tape wasn't something I enjoyed doing. I was desperate for one corner of my life to come back together so I certainly wasn't glad to read the words "Not good" in his email. But Ken also offered words of encouragement. He added that the voice was not damaged but my technique had fallen way off course. He encouraged me to work with Mark Oswald.

Julian Patrick was the next mentor to assist in my recovery. With surprising speed, Mark was able to get my voice back on solid ground. As if an announcement went out to the universe that I was able to sing again, I started to receive offers of work. It was like magic. I was hired to sing *The Barber of Seville* with a small company outside of Seattle and Julian demanded that I live at his house and take voice lessons with him every morning.

While it took some time to get back to the level I was at when I won the Metropolitan Opera auditions, this process made me a better singer than I would have been had I not experienced the breakdown. I learned much more about my voice and how it works. The experience actually raised the level of my abilities and increased my appreciation for the precious instrument that is my voice. The added bonus is that it has made me a more consistent and reliable singer. No matter what is happening in my personal life or what drama erupts during rehearsals, I can appreciate my colleagues and our ability to share music together.

As work started to come in, a friendlier universe seemed to come with it. There were unexpected surprises. I found myself appreciating the good breaks more than I had in the past. While flying home from Texas after performances of *Carmen* I boarded my flight and couldn't find my seat. The seat numbers started with numbers larger than those on my ticket. Was I on the wrong plane? There was a moment of panic which subsided with the welcome announcement confirming that I was on the right flight. I don't know how the upgrade happened, but I was booked in first class. I never flew first class before so I didn't look at the seat numbers until I was in coach.

I had no idea how I got a first class seat. I thought it was a mistake that would soon be corrected. Nevertheless, I sat there anyway. I hoped the mistake would go undetected and I would be able to remain in the seat for the entire flight. Before we took off, the nice flight attendant offered me a drink. I was still a bit paranoid about getting caught so I said no. NO? Once the plane was in the air, I managed to relax and accepted my free beer.

Do you feel like you're on the road to disaster with no idea how to get back on track? If we stand at the bottom of a mountain and look up at the massive climb ahead, it's possible we will stand there for years—frozen and overwhelmed. You could spend your time creating elaborate plans on how to pursue the perfect life. But those plans could be subject to change the moment they are made. Instead, I recommend taking one step, and then another, and then another. Eventually, you will be able to rest and enjoy the view. You will see that the view farther up the mountain is beautiful and at the same time, you will discover that it was the steps along the way that made the journey worthwhile.

> You never know how strong you are until being strong is the only choice you have. ~ Bob Marley.

Gratitude

> There is no greater power in the Universe than the power of love. The feeling of love is the highest frequency you can emit. If you could wrap every thought in love, if you could love everything and everyone, your life would be transformed.[16]

Living in New York City led to opportunities that I never would have had otherwise because it is one of the main international hubs of classical music. Living in New York led to my international debut in France in 2006.

A dear friend and fellow baritone who I first met in Seattle offered me his couch in New York City while I was between homes during my divorce. The help I received from my friend and his wife were paramount as I transitioned to my own apartment. Therefore, when he called me shortly after securing my new place, and asked if he could borrow my car I said yes.

His father had been in a motorcycle accident and he wanted to go take care of him. Parking in New York is a hassle so I felt he was doing me a favor by taking care of my car for a few days. I received a phone call with an update a couple of days later. The short story was that his father was fine and would make a full recovery. That was the good news. The bad news was that my friend was coming down with something and an appointment with his doctor was set for the next day. He was scheduled to fly to France in a few days, and he was concerned that his doctor might tell him that he couldn't travel. He asked if I was available and whether or not he could recommend me to cover for him. What an honor! Of course, I was available. What was the verdict from the doctor? My friend wasn't going anywhere.

---

[16] *The Secret.* Rhonda Byrne.

I received an email from the Lyrique en Mer Festival in Belle Isle, France. I knew they had little time to find a replacement singer and assumed they would look to hire someone closer to France. I considered this as nothing more than an opportunity to establish myself with the organization and hoped it would lead to a future engagement. All of the above went down by Friday afternoon.

By Sunday afternoon I heard nothing so I moved ahead with plans to secure a temporary work position in New York City. I had already interviewed with a temp agency and they set up a job for me on Monday morning. Before heading to the subway I left a voice mail for the festival in France saying that I assumed things had worked out with another singer but that I was still available if needed. With that, I headed to the first day of my new temp assignment with the Guggenheim Partners.

On the first day of my new job a meeting was scheduled with my boss at 9:00 am. I arrived five minutes early. He wasn't in the building yet. I was led to the reception area to wait. Sitting in the lounge, I considered the changes that might be in store with this new chapter in my life. Having just gone through a particularly wild set of changes I was somewhat apprehensive. Certainly, the rent had to be paid. I just hoped I would have the time required to continue my vocal studies.

At 9:02 the cell phone in my pocket buzzed. I checked the caller ID and it read "Unavailable call." I answered the phone. It was the general director for the festival in France.

"Keith, you're coming to France. Can you be on a plane tonight?"

I walked to the elevator, never met the boss, and left the building without speaking to anyone from the company. The ironic part is that I was to start this job one-week earlier, but for some reason the job was put on hold. Now that they were ready to move forward, I received an offer I could not refuse. When I called the temp agency they were super nice, wished me luck, and said to let them know when I was back in New York.

I knew that I would need time to study so I booked a flight for the following night. Fortunately, I had just updated my passport. Thinking back, it made no sense to renew my passport in June while I was in the middle of a contentious divorce (and had no money). But somehow I knew I needed to have a current passport and never thought twice about it. Now, only a few weeks after receiving my passport I was on my way to France for the first time in my life. I had also recently arranged for my bills to be paid online. I was prepared, so when opportunity came I was ready.

This turned out to be the longest trip to Europe ever and that was okay with me because my music score became a new physical appendage. My flight was to leave at 9:00 pm from JFK airport. The fight boarded on time and the plane pushed a few inches back when the captain's voice came over the intercom.

"Due to the power outage at La Guardia airport, air traffic is being sent here to JFK so there is a line for take-off. We should be in the air in about an hour."

The first hour and a half we sat on the tarmac with no water, no announcements, and no air conditioning. A plane full of hot sweaty passengers is not the best way to start a long trip.

Eventually, our plane moved to the runway and we were next in line for take-off. That's when the thunderstorm struck. Massive amounts of rain and wind slammed the entire area. Again, we had to wait, but at least we now had air conditioning. The total delay for take-off was four hours. I didn't mind the delays because I spent the entire time studying my music.

The original plan was to fly to Paris via Iceland, go directly to the train station, and head to Belle Isle. The four-hour delay changed everything.

I missed the connection in Iceland and was rerouted to Copenhagen. From Copenhagen I flew to Paris. At each stop, I called the festival office to let them know about the delays. They planned to meet me at the ferry when I arrived.

Ten hours later than scheduled, I finally arrived in Paris. The festival organizers set up a hotel room for me and changed my train ticket to the following day. All I had to do was find my way to the hotel. Being as familiar as I was with the New York City Subway system, how difficult could it be to travel by rail in Paris? At that time the ticketing machines were only in French and I barely knew where I was going. Fortunately, I met a guy in the ticket line who was about my age who was half French and half American. He was more than happy to help me make it into Paris safe and sound.

Once the RER made it into Paris my new friend told me to take the number 6 train to my final stop. I didn't know that the transfer from the RER to the number 6 required a new ticket. Having never navigated the tunnels before, I didn't know where I was going or where to buy the required ticket. Fortunately, someone left the gate open to the number 6 entrance. I assumed that using the gate was illegal, but I didn't see any other options. I passed through the gate and made it to my stop without punishment.

Luck was with me again when I reached my destination. Most subway stations in Paris require that you use your ticket to exit the station. This gives the authorities a second chance to catch gate jumpers. I didn't know this until I returned to Paris weeks later. Somehow I managed to exit the station without a ticket. Once on the sidewalk I realized that the only instructions I had were to go to the Hotel Ibis at this particular subway station. I didn't have an address and it was getting late. I began wondering if I was in a safe neighborhood. Well, a good look around is a good place to start, right? Standing on the street corner I slowly scanned the area with my jetlagged eyes. About two blocks away, slightly covered by the bushes, I saw the sign for the hotel. I was shocked and relieved. That was easy.

I arrived at the hotel around 10:30 in the evening and suddenly realized that this was my first time in *Paris*. It occurred to me that I might want to walk around and take in the sights. But I hadn't completely memorized my music so I opted for a review session before turning in. I never really went to bed. I fell asleep flat on my back, completely clothed, score at my side, and awoke in the same position the next morning. I panicked. I had no idea what time it was. There wasn't a clock in my room and I was sure I missed my train. I raced down to the reception desk and found it was exactly 7:00 am. My train didn't leave until noon. I could enjoy a little breakfast and plan my route to the train station.

Once on the train, I listened carefully to the announcements so I would know when to get off for the transfer. I needed to exit at Auray or I would be well on my way to getting lost. Having not studied French since Lawrence University I was admittedly rusty but when I heard the word "Auray" I made a quick exit. Standing on the platform, I looked in vain for my connection. I went inside and spoke to the ticket officer. The gentleman at the desk didn't speak English but he kindly tolerated my broken French. I managed to understand that I exited one stop too soon. Apparently, the conductor said "Auray, *next stop*."

Add two more hours to the delay. As I said, this was the longest trip ever. I made another call to the festival office; this was now beginning to feel like an international game of "Where's Waldo?" I caught the next train, made the transfer, found the bus at Quiberon to the ferry boat, and made the ferry just moments before it pushed off.

This fantastic adventure and four more seasons working for the same company are all thanks to my dear friend, David Adam Moore. David is a fantastic baritone who told me that he is thrilled to have been in a position to give my career such a boost. It is rare that singers who are in competition for the same roles are able to share work with each other.

How long did it take to learn and memorize the role of Ford in *Falstaff* for the festival in France? I memorized the entire show in six days with a total study time of 70 hours. This was the first of a number of emergencies in which I had to cover and memorize at the last minute. These quick studies are both scary and exhilarating at the same time. The wildest emergency I covered was for the role of Billy Bigelow in *Carousel*. I learned, memorized, and was on stage in 24 hours. That same company hired me a year later when they had yet another emergency. Harold Hill in the *Music Man* was memorized and staged in 48 hours. My third grade teacher would be blown away.

For my spirit and voice to completely heal there was one more musical element that I needed back in my life. Barbershop music. I had to have an outlet in my life that made music a labor of love and not just a competition for jobs—not just an obligation required to make financial ends meet. I wanted to return to my roots.

When I moved to Seattle to pursue my master's degree, I became inactive in Barbershop. I needed to focus my efforts on my studies and pursue high-level apprentice programs. Along the way, I forgot the reason I became a singer in the first place. My choral home and inspiration was found in the Westchester Chordsmen. It just so happens that at the time I needed them they were looking for a musical director. I auditioned and was offered the job the following day. While my chorus is proud to have a professional musician as their director, I don't think they ever knew that I needed them even more than they needed me. I am still their musical director today and this is the longest running position I have ever held.

Within a year of starting my position with the Chordsmen I made my debuts with the Metropolitan Opera, Carnegie Hall, Avery Fisher Hall (now David Geffen Hall), and received my first contract with the New York City Opera.

> When we experience acceptance, we have and enjoy everything as it is. We have no need to

change anything. It just is, and it's okay. It's beautiful just as it is.[17]

Dealing with Rejection

> You don't win or lose an audition. You build a career.[18]

In sales, you learn to deal with hearing the word "no," often. The gurus have all kinds of statistics as to how many no's you have to hear before you get a yes. While this can be very useful information, what is often overlooked is what all of those no's can do to your spirit. How do we survive through the mountain of rejection to find someone who will say "yes?"

From my Journal—August 9, 2011.

> I wonder sometimes if I resist truly believing unbelievably positive thoughts about myself because living in slight discomfort is better than living in complete disappointment.

Let's start with auditions. Auditions are how singers interview for jobs. Although singers are often advised that an audition is just another performance, auditioning is really not the same as performing. I think you can be good at both but being good at one does not mean you'll be good at the other. That is okay because auditions are just one way of securing a new client.

An audition is an opportunity in ten minutes or less to show what you are best at. Can you imagine if you interviewed for a job in corporate America and the ability to finish your interview rested on your photo and the first 30 seconds of that interview? You would say that is insane if not illegal. I don't have a better solution to the audition game but you can see why it's such a

---

[17] *The Sedona Method: Your Key to Lasting Happiness, Success, Peace and Emotional Well-being.* Hale Dwoskin and Jack Canfield.

[18] *Tales and Techniques of a Voiceover Actor* (2014). Harlan Hogan. Allworth Press.

high-pressure situation and how it can drive singers a bit crazy. This is why I say that auditions should just be one cog in your wheel when it comes to obtaining new clients.

In an opera, you have two or three hours to build a character and create an imaginary world for your audience. A few mistakes in a three-hour show are likely to be missed by an audience member. A few mistakes in an audition, especially within the first 30 seconds, can be deadly.

In an audition, you are singing for an audience that will often not give you a response, in an acoustical space that is less than ideal, and (more often than not) with a pianist you've never met. When does that ever happen in a real performance? Auditioning is not like a performance so don't treat it as if it is. This is where singers get confused. The game is different and you have to be able to accept a different kind of pressure. An audience member comes to a show to be entertained but an artistic director listens to an audition with an agenda to hire.

To properly apply for a position you need to prepare. Learn about the project for which you are applying, know the skills required, and understand what it is that *you* bring to the project. This brings me to a very important point. Never ever, ever, *ever* try to be what they want. Bring your real and natural self to an interview. The hiring bodies may or may not require your exact skills on the project. Remember that a high level application is never a "no;" it's often a "not at this time" or even a "not yet." If you take your true self to an audition you will leave proud of your performance. If you try and give them what you think they want you'll go insane trying to figure out who you should be and when you should be it.

Overcoming rejection is not about pleasing people or selling out. Overcoming rejection is about being true to yourself and finding those clients that see value in your product.

When you make-believe, the results come fast![19]

[19] *The Secret*. Rhonda Byrne.

Don't know where to start? Still building your skill set? Not sure your product is competitive yet? Many businesses experience these growing pains. Fake it until you make it. When you are uncertain of just what your truest self is, bring the life of preparation you have garnered up to today, and present it without apology. You will make your product better tomorrow. Not everyone who offers a rejection is an expert (or knows anything about the feedback they are giving). Filter feedback through your truest self and your intimate core of mentors. That will keep you motivated to improve.

> When it comes to innovation, Jobs is fond of quoting Picasso's famous dictum: good artists copy, great artists steal. To which Jobs adds: "And we have always been shameless about stealing great ideas."[20]

The truth is you are not a mind reader so you never really know what anyone is thinking. I have sung auditions where I received rave reviews but didn't get a contract and auditions where they didn't even say hello to me but offered me a job.

> Don't listen to your customers. They don't know what they want.[21]

I sang for the first time in Israel during the summer of 2017. As part of this trip, I had high hopes of auditioning for the Israeli Opera and adding a bucket-list contract to my resume. Through connections at the summer festival I was able to obtain an audition with Michael Ajzenstadt, a kind man with a brilliantly discerning ear. Michael has a historian's mind for opera.

This was the opportunity I was waiting for and a major reason why I accepted a slot in the summer festival. The audition took place in a small room, with a pianist I never met. As soon as I began, Michael started texting. Oh, boy. This cannot be good. He's already bored. When I completed the first aria he finished his text and said "That was nice. What else did you bring?"

---

[20] *Inside Steve's Brain*. Leander Kahney.
[21] Ibid.

Most opera singers get to sing two arias in an audition so asking for a second aria was common practice and didn't necessarily indicate interest. The texting continued through the second aria and as I approached the end he picked up the phone and started to make a phone call. This was clearly bad. Now he was so bored he was making a phone call while I sang!

He spoke in Hebrew during the phone call so I had no idea what was happening. When he hung up he explained that he invited a colleague to hear me. Would I mind singing a couple more arias when she arrived? What a turn-around! You don't invite a colleague and extend an audition if you have lost interest. My energy picked up and I sang two more arias before heading back to rehearsal at the summer festival.

As soon as I arrived at rehearsal the conductor who set up the audition gave me a big hug and said,

"He loved you."

"Really? I wasn't sure. He was texting the whole time."

"Yeah. He was texting me."

You really never know. Two days later Michael offered me my debut with the Israeli Opera as Albert in *Werther*.

By representing your true self in an interview you will be more relaxed and you will be laying the groundwork for the future. Contracts can be offered when least expected. I have had auditions that booked three years after the audition. In fact, the first time that happened the artistic director talked about how he enjoyed my audition three years prior and finally had the right project for me. I wrote that one off as a bad audition that never booked. I was wrong.

A good audition today might cause someone to watch you and keep track of your progress before hiring you. In some cases you'll know this and in others you won't. Remember this important rule once again: Success is when preparation meets opportunity. You have 100% control over your preparation.

> I have had lots of help along the way, but my most valuable tools, perhaps even more than natural

talent, have been persistence and consistent hard work. I did the work required to get myself prepared, then I simply refused to go away. Eventually, the industry gave up and let me come in to play, and for this, I am grateful. If you love this stuff, don't let anything stop you.[22]

The legendary cellist, Pablo Casals, was asked why he continued to practice at age 90. He replied,

"Because I think I'm making progress."

One extremely cold December day, I auditioned for the Santa Fe Opera Young Artist Program in New York City. I was on a roll having just won a vocal competition and my auditions that season were going very well. I sang one aria and when I was done the company representatives said I sounded great but did not ask for a second aria. Then something surprising happened. The pianist, who was hired by the company for the audition (someone I had never met before), offered me a job. He was hiring for a concert in New York City and thought I was exactly the kind of baritone he was looking for. This would not be the last time I booked a job for something other than the one for which I was auditioning.

To judge your life or anyone else's, your progress or the seeming lack thereof, by any spot along the path takes whatever's happening in that moment completely out of context.[23]

Competition. The world seems to thrive on it. The winner is a hero and the loser is—well—a loser. Modern television has turned the singing competition on its head. Sometimes these competitions exploit the performer by publically embarrassing them in the name of entertainment. Other times they serve as a springboard for a successful career. The opera world is full of competitions.

[22] *Tales and Techniques of a Voiceover Actor*. Harlan Hogan.
[23] *The Top Ten Things Dead People Want to Tell YOU*. Mike Dooley. ©Mike Dooley, www.tut.com

Why don't we always agree with who wins? Do the judges lack talent? Can't they see how great the *loser* is? Music is an art and every person is going to value different attributes. You like Picasso and I like Monet. Which one is better? You would argue Picasso is the grand master. So it is with all art forms. That is why we must not lose our spirit by over thinking how the judges reach their decisions. Be true to yourself and you will always be a winner—no matter who actually wins a particular competition.

Although winning a contest can help a singer's career it certainly does not guarantee one. To illustrate this just look at the list of winners from any major competition on TV or otherwise and ask yourself how many of these singers are still singing today? Contests can offer singers excellent exposure but building a business is quite different.

In 2002, I won a small vocal competition in Longview, Texas that led to more singing work than any of the other competitions I ever won. The contest took place in three rounds. Round one consisted of sending in an application with a recording. Once accepted, the finalists traveled to Longview for the final two rounds of competition sung live in front of a panel of judges. All 20 singers performed on Friday and the top ten performed on Saturday. There were some very fine performances that weekend and I was honored to receive the top award.

I wasn't sure how soon the events of the weekend would wrap up so I booked my flight home for Sunday. As it turned out, I was the only singer left in town and was invited to dinner with the judges. The conversation eventually turned to the contest itself and the difficulty of being a judge. There was one judge who single handedly was in charge of screening all the recordings from round one. He asked the managing director if there were any surprises in the contest. "Yes," she replied. "You cut Keith."

Initially, I had not made the cut and was not going to be invited to the finals in Texas. But the managing director liked my head shot and said she had a feeling about me that she could not explain so she invited me anyway.

Vocal competitions of this nature are often judged based on opinion rather than math. That is to say that after the contest is over the judges go into a private room and argue their case for the winner. The managing director wanted none of that and created a scoring system for the judges. Once the contest was over she did the math and the winners were announced.

The math was quite simple. Each judge would pick their top five singers:

1 point for fifth place;
2 points for fourth place;
3 points for third place;
4 points for second place; and
5 points for first place

What makes my cut during the first round even more interesting is that I won the contest by a large margin. The managing director said I finished first or second with every judge, which is very uncommon. It is so uncommon that I was the only singer in the top ten that all the judges had finishing in the top five.

For fun, the managing director took out the judge's notes from the prerecorded session. As he re-read his remarks he smiled at me and said "I didn't hear any of this in your voice this weekend."

I never asked to see his notes but I did ask if maybe my recording was bad. He laughed and said "I wouldn't worry about it. This just goes to show you how subjective this business is. Today you won. Enjoy it and enjoy the relationships you have made in Longview."

Competition is an example of separation. First, when you have thoughts of competition, it is coming from a lack of mentality, as you are saying there is a limited supply. You are saying there is not enough for everybody, so we have to compete and fight to get things.[24]

Sometimes the spirit of competition can be great fun. While I was an apprentice at Santa Fe Opera I sang *The Lord's Prayer* for the First United Methodist Church in Santa Fe one Sunday morning. This inspirational song is powerful with a dramatic ending and to my complete shock the congregation gave me a standing ovation. That never happens during a church service. The pastor got up to give his sermon and said "Wow! That usually only happens after my sermons."

Dealing with rejection also means being honest when you make a mistake and taking ownership of your actions. While living in Seattle, I accidentally double booked myself and was almost fired from a concert. Seattle Opera engaged me to sing a Thursday evening concert and I was also hired to sing a Cantata for a church that following Sunday morning. The conflict came up in rehearing for the Sunday morning cantata. The only rehearsal with the orchestra was Thursday evening.

I wrote the music director explaining my conflict and asked if I could come early Sunday morning to rehearse. He didn't appreciate playing second fiddle to what appeared to be a much more important job and said he was considering hiring another singer. I immediately wrote back agreeing with his point of view. I explained that this was my mistake, his rehearsal was a priority, and asked if I could recommend an appropriate singer as my replacement. The music director was stunned and because I did away with the need for a battle, he responded that I was the singer he wanted. He agreed to find a way to make a Sunday morning rehearsal work.

Always treat everyone you meet with respect. You never know who you are meeting or who will be watching.

---

[24] *The Secret*. Rhonda Byrne.

The final and most important aspect in dealing with rejection is to love yourself. You must love yourself first before you can sincerely share your love with others. When you are true to yourself you can perform without veils and your personality shines at its brightest. When you hide and are not true to yourself your purpose fades and loss and insecurity take over. Know that you already are enough and are worth infinitely more than you can ever imagine. So imagine big.

> By acknowledging our gifts and skills we operate from an "I have" mind-set rather than an "I need to get" mentality.[25]

---

[25] *Life Visioning: A Transformative Process for Activating Your Unique Gifts and Highest Potential.* Michael Bernard Beckwith and Bruce H. Lipton.

Kevin Eutsler and Keith Harris, New Haven, CT 2018

Nerves and Stage Fright

Fear is the enemy of creativity.[26]

Do you suffer from nerves and stage fright? Let's get to the heart of this right now.

> Nerve: a person's mental state, in particular the extent to which they are agitated or worried.

> Nerves: brace oneself mentally to face a demanding situation.

Both of these common definitions suggest that nerves, by nature, are a negative state and I believe this is where we go wrong. Nerves and stage fright belong in two different categories. Let's start with nerves.

Nerves are a form of energy. People often ask me if I get nervous before a performance and I respond by saying if I'm not nervous that means that I don't care. Nerves can provide a great source of energy and focus. Unfortunately, we only feel this when we are under pressure. The body instinctively knows when we need an increase in adrenalin to take on a high-pressure task and responds accordingly; singing to a theater full of people, for example. Because this heightened state is only felt when we are under pressure, it makes us very uncomfortable and we immediately judge that feeling as negative. Such a massive explosion of energy cannot be suppressed and left unfocused. It finds its own outlet. This is why someone under great pressure can experience uncontrollable shakes, physical trembles, or shortness of breath.

While beta-blockers and similar attempts at therapy are designed to make a performer more comfortable, performers who truly own the stage should never be completely comfortable. A comfortable performer is unmemorable. A great performer holds our attention like a wild animal. Popular opinion supports

---

[26] *Tales and Techniques of a Voiceover Actor*. Harlan Hogan

that the wild animal was born under a star and while I would agree that talents like John Lennon or Steven Tyler were born for fame, anyone who learns how to tap into their nerves can become a wild animal in their profession.

How do we deal with these uncomfortable sensations? The most important step is to stop judging them. A friend of mine who helps singers with nerves received a phone call from a client who was in an absolute hysteria.

"I am having a panic attack."

"How do you know?"

"My heart is racing, my breath is short, and I am sweating."

"Are you sure you're not having an orgasm?"

The physical descriptions for an orgasm and the supposed panic attack are the same. What changes is our response to each. We judge one sensation response as positive and the other as negative. What would happen if you just let the butterflies float around in your gut? How bad could it really be? This same friend is also a conductor who performed for years on Broadway. Even after hundreds of shows he still gets nervous. He found his preshow jitters so uncomfortable that he finally put a sign on his music stand that said "Fine. Go ahead and die then."

While a bit dramatic, and hopefully hilarious to the people sitting in the front row, the point he was making to himself was that his nerves really weren't something that should ruin his night. He could handle a few uncomfortable sensations in his body. Over time, he noticed that his best performances happened when he was nervous.

> We live in a world of assumptions, thinking we are relating to facts. In some ways, our feelings are just stories that we have made up about a particular set of sensations. These stories often, if not always, come after the feeling has already arisen in our consciousness. We then use them to explain why we feel the way we feel.[27]

---

[27] *The Sedona Method: Your Key to Lasting Happiness, Success, Peace and Emotional Well-being.* Hale Dwoskin and Jack Canfield.

When I am backstage, if my heart doesn't race, my stomach doesn't jump, or my hands don't sweat, that is when I really get *nervous* because I am not excited to perform. Carrying nerves is a little bit like exercise. Sore muscles don't feel good at first but over time the endorphin rush motivates people to continue to stay fit. Making friends with my uncomfortable backstage physical sensations has now lead to a response of "all systems go." If I feel ill backstage I know it will be a great show.

Does this mean I walk around backstage sick and terrified? Not at all. As I mentioned earlier, carrying a heavy weight emotionally is a lot like carrying a heavy weight at the gym. If you do it enough times, it doesn't seem so heavy after a while. Over time, I realized that adrenalin is a powerful source of energy that helps me communicate better with my audience.

From my journal—December 14, 2001.

Think all you want BEFORE you get on stage.

How do we tap into this wealth of terrifying energy? Through visualization and preparation. Everyone has a constant, on-going inner monologue. We can't escape it, but we can program it for success. We do this by visualizing the event before it happens. Close your eyes, imagine yourself on stage or in your state of nervousness. Picture yourself using that energy to excel at your task.

The next step is to clean up your inner monologue. It's imperative that we retrain the little devil that sits on our shoulder and tells us everything we are doing wrong as we do it. I encourage people to think in terms of verbs or actions. What are you doing—actually doing in that moment? Do not get confused. Being is not a state of doing. Being happy will not work but celebrating will. If you fill your head with action verbs two things happen:

1. You're more likely to stay in the moment; and
2. There isn't any room for negative self-judgment.

Visualize how the performance will go and trust your preparation once you get on stage.

No matter what profession you are in there is a lot to be said for repetition and muscle memory. When our mind goes blank the muscle memory or preparation takes over and your audience will never know the difference.

I was performing the role of Dandini in *La Cenerentola* (Cinderella) in Seattle. In this version of Cinderella, Dandini, the valet to the prince, is given the task of pretending he is the prince so that the prince can travel incognito and find his true love. My first entrance in the show is grand as I enter showing off my power and the first lines sung are my aria. Opening night, I walked on stage, looked at the conductor, and my mind went blank. I had completely forgotten the first words.

The conductor smiled, cued me to sing, and sound came out of my mouth. My body started singing even though I had completely forgotten my lines. About two lines later I caught up with myself and realized everything was going quite well.

After the show I spoke to the conductor.

> "Wow! That was scary. When I came on stage my mind went blank."
> "Yeah, I know. That was funny."
> "Well, why didn't you toss me a line?"

I will never forget his response. Maestro Dean Williamson said,

> "I knew you didn't need it because I know how you practice."

Dean knew that my practice habits were grounded so deeply in repetition and muscle memory that when I looked at him with blank shark eyes he was cool and calm. My preparation took care of me while I was still learning how to focus my adrenalin rush.

That ownership is the key to releasing our fears and insecurities, accepting our gifts and abilities, and rediscovering the original passions that were given to us at birth. Having rediscovered that essential nature, we can endeavor to act with integrity in every aspect of life. No one does that perfectly or completely; the value is in the pursuit.[28]

Stage fright is a state of mind and while it often feels a lot like nerves, stage fright is caused by actual fear because something is actually wrong. Being under pressure causes nerves but having technical issues causes stage fright. For singers, this often comes in the form of vocal insecurity and the only solution is to sing better. If you don't know what sounds are going to come out of your mouth you have every right to be scared. This happens to me when I perform under the weather. While my technique takes care of me and I have never crashed and burned on stage, performing when you do not feel well causes great insecurity.

Pushing out, out, out. Now, that also has a great residual to it. That will take away stage fright in two seconds. Excuse me . . . that won't take the fright away, but that will take the shake away.[29] ~ Marilyn Horne, internationally renowned mezzo-soprano.

Everyone suffers from insecurity at some point and the most insecure feeling is thinking something is wrong. The common response is to retreat and block the issue. See no evil hear no evil. I have found, however, that sticking my head right into the center of the pain and accepting my part in it helps melt away the stage fright. We might not be able to change the situation, but we can

[28] *The Naked Voice: A Wholistic Approach to Singing.* W. Stephen Smith and Michael Chipman.

[29] *Great Singers on Great Singing: A Famous Opera Star Interviews 40 Famous Opera Singers on the Technique of Singing.* Jerome Hines.

be our own best friend and offer a hug to the scared child inside us.

Doing so will make you a better colleague too because another common response to insecurity is to demand that others make changes in order to make us happy. This never goes over well and doesn't solve the heart of the issue either. Controlling what others think and do in order to validate my insecurities ends up driving me insane, and does nothing to relieve those insecurities.

Which is also saying, if you love what you do don't sabotage yourself by blaming others. This tactic sidetracks us and makes sure we're never quite available for the success we think we deserve. Anything you wish to do well needs your time and attention without reservation.

> Another reason many people are hesitant when they begin letting go of feelings is the belief that feelings give them important information and intuition. In my experience, the opposite is true.[30]

Hokan Hakagard, a wonderful baritone from Sweden, describes two kinds of performers. He says there are performers who like the lights on and those who like the lights off. The lights on people are those who like to see the audience and speak directly to their listeners. The lights off people prefer to not see the audience and perform the message through larger physical gestures.

Regardless of which kind of performer you are, the synergy or interaction between the performer and audience is the ultimate goal. This happens when the performer inspires an audience, they feed the performer in return and a beautiful circle of energy is created. I don't know how to describe that feeling but when it happens everyone participating knows it. The atmosphere of the room becomes magical. It may only be for a moment; nothing else matters but the relationship between the performer and the

---

[30] *The Sedona Method: Your Key to Lasting Happiness, Success, Peace and Emotional Well-being.* Hale Dwoskin and Jack Canfield.

audience. The groundwork for this exchange comes from visualization. See it then do it.

> Intuition is actually the natural knowing of our true
> nature that gets obstructed by emotions.[31]

There were two performances in my life when I actually thought about not walking on stage. The first time was when I performed my master's recital at the University of Washington and the second was when I made my Seattle Opera debut. As I stood backstage moments before my entrance to both performances, I thought "What would happen if I just went home right now?"

The answer that immediately came to mind was that I would never sing again. Whether it was stage fright, nerves or a combination of both, I forced myself to walk on stage one step at a time, and I am alive today to tell the story. Taking that first single step was the hardest. Even when we prepare there will be times we simply need a little push to see it through. When that moment comes and you're standing backstage wondering how to proceed, my advice is to stop thinking and just walk on stage.

I've also had two days in my life where I thought about a career change. I questioned whether or not I could stomach the life of a singer and wondered if I should keep going. In reality, I was questioning my personal value and my ability to compete. My wife was the one who talked me through this crisis and I am singer today because of my wife, Maire. She talked me through my fears and helped me stay focused on my dreams. She would not allow me to lower my standards or accept defeat over a little frustration or fear. After many hours of discussion, her support came down to "Stay put. You're right where you belong." She was absolutely right.

---

[31] *The Sedona Method: Your Key to Lasting Happiness, Success, Peace and Emotional Well-being.* Hale Dwoskin and Jack Canfield.

Without her love and support it's quite possible I would have, once again, lost my way, allowed my purpose fade, and found myself searching to find my voice.

> Wanna-bes and new-bes may think that eventually it all gets easy: The phone starts ringing and never stops. I wish that were true. It's not. Still, the ride is worth it, believe me.[32]

From my journal—December 11, 2003.

> It's been a wild ride. While the growth is inspiring, I am understanding why they are called growing pains.

---

[32] *Tales and Techniques of a Voiceover Actor*. Harlan Hogan.

Effort and Reward

> Follow your heart. This is your purpose. You have
> desires; admit them. Listen to them. Choose to
> bring them to life. Your dreams are yours for a
> reason: to make them come true.[33]

Let's go back now to a period about 15 years after I graduated from Lawrence University. It was at this point that I was singing professionally, made my Metropolitan Opera and European debuts, and had sung at Carnegie Hall as a principle soloist. I had learned to work with my dyslexia, and developed an ability to memorize large scores of music quickly making me popular for emergency work whenever a singer canceled at the last minute.

About this same time, I was contracted to sing the baritone solos for the *Carmina Burana* in Lancaster, Pennsylvania. As stated earlier, the *Carmina Burana* is a massive work for baritone. This particular weekend challenged my vocal limits as never before because the engagement required me to perform this work four times in three days. There was a concert Friday evening, two concerts on Saturday and one on Sunday afternoon. The Lancaster Symphony Orchestra sold out every performance.

The symphony's conductor mentioned that he was good friends with the dean of the Lawrence University Conservatory. As such, Dean Dodson and his wife would be attending the concert. This was a wonderful surprise because they were both very supportive of me during my Lawrence years. Knowing they would be there brought back fond memories of Lawrence and the vocal recovery that lead me to this concert. I was determined to give them an exciting evening of music.

---

[33] *The Top Ten Things Dead People Want to Tell YOU*. Mike Dooley. ©Mike Dooley, www.tut.com

After a wonderful concert, we went out to dinner and after the small talk had settled, Dean Dodson's wife, Alberta, turned to me and said "Did you know you were almost not accepted into Lawrence?"

This was the first time anyone ever told me this. I immediately said "My ACT score?" She nodded. I smiled back "Yeah, it wasn't so good."

Alberta laughed and said "Oh my, no it wasn't." Then she told me that she was in the room when the college and the conservatory fought over me. The college said they could not possibly accept someone with such a low ACT score, but the conservatory argued that my high school grades were good and I could sing.

Then Alberta deepened her focus. "Do you know that today Lawrence University no longer requires an ACT score with their applications?"

I had no idea how closely I was being watched while I was a student and how both the college and the conservatory were privately celebrating my success and the success of other students like me. So much so that Lawrence changed the application process to be sure they could enroll more *dumb* kids like me. The best part of the story is that I never knew any of this. I am certainly not the only student Lawrence took a chance on and it's inspiring to see this wave of change taking place in colleges nationwide.

> You happen to life. Everything happens for a reason. You are untouchable by others, and you are the Creator of your experiences.[34]

We all want to feel like we're making a difference in the world and doing something meaningful that will leave a mark on society.

---

[34] *The Top Ten Things Dead People Want to Tell YOU*. Mike Dooley. ©Mike Dooley, www.tut.com

We have such a need for immediate gratification that if we don't see our mission progress, in our own way, we assume it's not happening. I got into college because I wanted to sing, and by being true to myself and what I knew was right for me in my gut. I was part of a movement that was much larger than me, and much more important than I could have imagined.

> When the music changes the temple shakes. ~
> Plato.

Don't try to do life right. Take a note from Frank Sinatra: "I did it my way."

When I became a singer I refused to claim the title of "Starving Artist." Instead, I was determined to be an entrepreneur who sings. While singing pulls the train, this shift in business psychology has allowed me to keep adding new product offerings for my clients and puts me in control of my business. Don't know where to start? Who cares? Do something. Do anything. My mom became a social worker to figure out that she wanted to be a Minister. Was that a mistake or a misstep? Or was it the experience she needed to find her higher calling? The only way to mess up progress is to literally do nothing at all.

> The things that come to those that wait may be the
> things left by those that got there first.[35]

You might have talent. Clearly, I have an affinity for singing. But talent is only 10% of the game. Your work ethic is the other 90%. So even if you think you don't have any talent, you still have the option to choose how you develop that special 90%. What if you're wrong about not having any talent? Maybe you actually do have some and suddenly you're now at 95%. My parents gave me a poster when I was in middle school. The picture was of a sprinter going over a hurdle and the caption said "If you cannot win, make the person ahead of you break the record."

---

[35] *Does the Noise in My Head Bother You?* Steven Tyler.

> You often feel tired, not because you've done too much, but because you've done too little of what sparks a light in you. ~ Alexander den Heijer.

Do we give our true unfiltered selves enough credit? How often are we making a difference because of who we are and not just because of what we do? I got into Lawrence simply because my spirit told me to sing. The logistics worked themselves out. I hope my story offers a glimpse into how we are all worth infinitely more than we imagine. Even if you think you are the dumb kid in the room and you find yourself fighting roadblock after roadblock, don't be afraid to imagine big. Quite likely you're already a part of something even bigger.

> The liberated individual who has realized the Self and Spirit within him, who has entered into the cosmic consciousness ... acts by the light and energy of the Power within him working through his human instruments.[36]

---

[36] *Life Visioning: A Transformative Process for Activating Your Unique Gifts and Highest Potential*. Michael Bernard Beckwith and Bruce H. Lipton.

Love Yourself

> What quantum physicists and Einstein tell us is that everything is happening simultaneously. If you can understand that there is no time, and accept that concept, then you will see that whatever you want in the future already exists.[37]

Although American pop culture glorifies the overnight superstar wunderkind who was apparently born for fame, life is not a race. Success requires many years of daily preparation. In the opera business, one of the dream companies to work for is the Metropolitan Opera. I have always had good experiences working at the Met and there is almost always a famous person in the hall getting ready for a performance. History and excitement resonate from the building. Julian Patrick made his Metropolitan Opera debut at the age of 62. Fans of his announced with pride, that Julian was a baritone of the Metropolitan Opera. No one ever said "yeah, but he didn't get there until he was 62."

Julian obviously didn't start singing at age 60 either. Value the little prizes along the way. Often, we're so focused on the big goal we forget to enjoy the little victories that lead to the big goal. The famous answer to the question "How do you get to Carnegie Hall" is "practice, practice, practice." We say this because practice makes perfect. Right? But if practice made perfect wouldn't perfection be easy? Practice makes permanent. Permanence is like creating a habit and good habits can take years to master.

While you're mastering your skills remember to take a day off now and again. There is much more to life than business. A healthy person needs to stay balanced and we all need a hobby. All work and no play will eventually cause your creativity and your motivation to fade. We all have different talents and interests,

---

[37] *The Secret*. Rhonda Byrne.

joys and influences. Too easily we become worn down by the daily grind. But even those mundane daily tasks can become more fulfilling with the right mental attitude and a little rejuvenation.

> Everyone should find at least one passion or hobby that you absolutely love doing and let that be your escape. Euphoria is a state that is not often reached, but when you feel it you cannot mistake it and it forces you to smile inwardly and outwardly!
> ~ Lawrence Brownlee, internationally renowned operatic tenor.

Fitness has become one of my hobbies because it gives me a feeling of immediate gratification. Once you've completed a physical exercise you cannot give it back. The work is done and the muscles have performed that task. The body will now rebuild muscle tissue while you sleep. What a brilliant pay off for a little bit of sweat. Fitness is also an active metaphor for life. Each moment in life is an experience that will continue to grow even while you sleep. Want the most out those experiences? Appreciate all of them without judgment. Doing so will allow you to pursue your dreams and goals with a sense of purpose each day and without getting sidetracked by complaining about what you believe you deserve.

> The adventure of life is every bit the school of life.
> The more you learn, the more fun you can have;
> the more fun you have, the more you can learn.[38]

I am sure you are familiar with the phrase "to get up on the wrong side of bed."

We take that to mean someone is in a bad mood. But have you ever stopped to notice how that mood developed? Let's say, for example, that you wake up flushed because your alarm was set incorrectly. You scramble out of bed, stub your toe on the

---

[38] *The Top Ten Things Dead People Want to Tell YOU*. Mike Dooley. ©Mike Dooley, www.tut.com

corner of the dresser, scream out, survey the damage, and accept defeat (even the dresser is stronger than you are). This leads to breakfast spilling on your clothes, which leads to leaving late for work because you had to change, which leads to arriving late for work. The day starts to spin out of control and before you know it you're in an awful mood because you "got up on the wrong side of bed." Life is apparently against you.

Take a breath and take in the moment. Maybe you needed the extra sleep? But if I get to work late I might lose my job. Maybe that is the push you needed to find your real calling. But I worry and this, that, and the other. How many of the worries that you carry actually ever come to fruition? Every moment in life can be received with a variety of perspectives. "Life is against me" is a perspective that takes away your power and is defeating. "Maybe it's time for a career change," on the other hand, is empowering and puts you back in the driver's seat.

From my journal—December 11, 2003.

There have been so many events in my life that I saw happen many years before they actually did happen.

Patience does not come easily for most of us but can be developed by appreciating those little moments. Especially the ones that seem to happen by accident.

Social media quickly misguides our sense of reality and patience. A quick rundown on Instagram and you think everyone else is happy and successful. You are the only one struggling and having to work so hard each day. This single thought made me wonder who else shares my struggles. So I did something, for this book, that I never did before. I did a Google search for famous people with dyslexia. Here are just a few of the names I found:

Henry Winkler
Leonardo da Vinci
Walt Disney

Albert Einstein
John F Kennedy
John Lennon
Steven Spielberg

That is one heck of a list of kids we certainly would not consider *dumb*.

Man becomes what he thinks about.[39]

My stepfather, Russ, was a Methodist Minister. A brilliant storyteller, his sermons were more like inspirational speeches than biblical lessons. Once his stories had drawn people in and the lessons were taught he would end his sermons with a simple but powerful question that has stayed with me.

How is it with your life?

What I learned is that it's not enough to just enjoy or understand the story. For those lessons to impact your life you have to take action and only you get to decide what that action is and how you take it. Life is a participation sport and all the people in it are your teammates, or as we say in the theatre "life is not a dress rehearsal, this is the performance." Work up a sweat, take a bow, applaud your friends, and bring the best you can offer on that day. Every single experience in life has made you who you are today.

How is it with your life? ~ Russ May, 1941-2015.

---

[39] *The Secret.* Rhonda Byrne.

About the Author

Keith Harris is an American Baritone, who has been captivating audiences in his performances on both operatic and concert stages. Performance highlights include the Metropolitan Opera House, Israeli Opera, New York City Opera, Teatro Comunale di Bologna, The Festival Lyrique International de Belle-Île en Mer in France, Toledo Opera, Opera Tampa, Opera Carolina, Seattle Opera, Santa Fe Opera, Opera Theatre of Saint Louis, Holders Festival in Barbados, Nevada Opera, Opera of East Texas, El Paso Opera, Annapolis Opera, Mobile Opera, and Skagit Opera.

His vast operatic repertoire includes the roles of Count Almaviva in *Le nozze di Figaro,* Dandini in *La Cenerentola,* the début of the role Sir Plume in the world première of *The Rape of the Lock,* Valentin in *Faust,* Silvio and Tonio in *Pagliacci,* Albert in *Werther,* Belcore in *L'elisir d'amore*, Iago in *Otello*, Ford in *Falstaff*, Guglielmo in *Così fan tutte*, Figaro in *Il barbiere di Siviglia*, Escamillo in *Carmen*, Papageno in *Die Zauberflöte*, and Athanaël in *Thaïs*. Mr. Harris has also performed the musical theater role of Billy Bigelow in *Carousel*, Anthony Hope in *Sweeney Todd*, Pirate Bras Pique in *Naughty Marietta*, and Harold Hill in *The Music Man.*

Keith Harris, a seasoned concert artist, has also appeared in performance with numerous esteemed symphonies throughout North America. He made his Carnegie Hall début in 2009, singing the world première of David N. Child's *Requiem*. As a regular performer at Carnegie Hall, he has performed great works such as Hayes' *Te Deum*, Haydn's *Lord Nelson Mass*, Orff's *Carmina Burana*, and Rutter's *Mass of the Children*. Other works in Mr. Harris' concert repertoire include; Beethoven's *Symphony No. 9,* Fauré's *Requiem*, Haydn's *Heiligmesse,* Ed Lojeski's *Psalms of Passover*, Händel's *Messiah*, Gerald Finzi's *In Terra Pax,* and Argento's *Andrée Expedition.* Mr. Harris has also performed in major halls, such as New York City's David Geffen Hall (previously called Avery Fisher Hall) and Alice Tully Hall, Seattle's Benaroya Hall, Savannah's Mercer Hall, London's Cadogan Hall and more.

After reading this bio, yes, go ahead and ask. When did he have time to write a book?

To top this question and because he is not busy enough, Harris also created a one-man show and inspirational presentation combining music and his vast performance experience to compliment his unique story.

Schools, churches, and corporations are using his message to help people find the advantage in their disadvantage.

For booking, recordings and his performance schedule please visit: www.KeithHarrisOpera.com.

34335534R00076

Made in the USA
Middletown, DE
29 January 2019